Graeme Turner AO is Professor Emeritus of Cultural Studies at the University of Queensland, Australia. He is one of the founding figures of media and cultural studies in Australia, and a leading figure internationally. He has been writing about Australian media, culture and society for many years, with a continuing focus on the idea of the nation. He has published over twenty-nine books, including *Making It National* (1994), *Ending the Affair: The decline of Australian television news and current affairs* (2005), *Re-inventing the Media* (2016) and *Essays in Media and Cultural Studies: In transition* (2020). His most recent book is *John Farnham's Whispering Jack* (2022).

THE
SHRINKING
NATION

How we got here and
what can be done about it

GRAEME TURNER

First published 2023 by University of Queensland Press
PO Box 6042, St Lucia, Queensland 4067 Australia

University of Queensland Press (UQP) acknowledges the Traditional Owners and their custodianship of the lands on which UQP operates. We pay our respects to their Ancestors and their descendants, who continue cultural and spiritual connections to Country. We recognise their valuable contributions to Australian and global society.

uqp.com.au
reception@uqp.com.au

Cover design by Josh Durham (Design By Committee)
Cover photograph by Alamy / Josh Durham
Author photograph by Russell Shakespeare
Typeset in 12/16 pt Bembo Std by Post Pre-press Group, Brisbane
Printed in Australia by McPherson's Printing Group

University of Queensland Press is assisted by the Australian Government through the Australia Council, its arts funding and advisory body.

A catalogue record for this book is available from the National Library of Australia.

ISBN 978 0 7022 6619 5 (pbk)
ISBN 978 0 7022 6802 1 (epdf)
ISBN 978 0 7022 6803 8 (epub)

University of Queensland Press uses papers that are natural, renewable and recyclable products made from wood grown in well-managed forests and other controlled sources. The logging and manufacturing processes conform to the environmental regulations of the country of origin.

Contents

'It just feels like Australia has shrunk'

Australia has been experiencing a sustained period of accelerated sociocultural change, accompanied by existential threats from natural disasters and the Covid-19 pandemic, and punctuated by repeated cycles of political upheaval. A great deal of what has occurred over the last decade and a half has been socially and culturally divisive, fracturing bonds of community and identity while frustrating the aspiration to move towards a positive and informed consensus about the kind of nation and society we wish to create. Indeed, it seems at times as if the capacity to adapt, to compromise, to progress or reform, and to rationally address the most urgent issues dividing our communities is simply beyond us. Our politicians, in particular, appear to have 'forgotten how to govern'.[1]

For some years now, pollsters have been telling us that Australians have become increasingly concerned about the state of their nation, and disappointed by what Australia has become.[2] The success of independent candidates during the 2022 federal election constitutes one response to that disappointment, but it is reflected more widely in repeated iterations of the phrase

'We should be better than this' in relation to the handling of gender equity in the workplace and in the courts, the failure to address Indigenous disadvantage, and the fear that Australia has become 'an international pariah' over inaction on climate change and punitive policies on refugees. Indeed, over the years 2019 to 2022 in particular, there has been a swelling chorus of frustration from all quarters of the commentariat at the stalled progress on a wide range of pressing political concerns, at the failure of government service delivery at both state and federal levels, and at the deteriorating ethical standards on display in the hyper-partisan performance of contemporary politics.[3] More broadly, Australians' disappointment has focused upon how the culture of politics in Australia has changed, most significantly since the election of the government of Kevin Rudd in 2007. This book characterises that sense of disappointment as the perception that the nation has 'shrunk': that it is now less than it was, and less than it should be.

This perception is not only a product of Australians' experience of the pandemic – although Covid has certainly generated major disruptions that feed into it. These include the insular retreat into 'Fortress Australia', the federal government's refusal to honour Australia's obligations to citizens stranded offshore, the fractious fragmentation of the nation into states and regions, and the escalating concerns about the compromised competence and political short-termism of (especially, but not exclusively) the federal government. However, our experience of the pandemic has only served to expose fault lines in Australian politics, culture and society that were already there. Well before Covid arrived, many Australians had found that the state was failing them.[4] Not only that, but many Australians also suspected that those charged with preserving the national wellbeing held a diminished sense of responsibility for that task: hence the simmering resonance of

2

former prime minister Scott Morrison's disastrous defence during the bushfire crisis of 2019–20: 'I don't hold a hose, mate.'

This book would be far from alone in suggesting that instead of rising to the social and political challenges of the last decade or so – climate change, natural disasters, the housing crisis, predatory behaviour in the financial services industries, gender inequity in the workplace and male violence in the home, the buckling structures of aged care and social welfare – our leaders have largely ducked them. Indeed, *The Shrinking Nation* responds to a widening concern that where the nation may once have generated a confident sense of legitimacy, a convincing moral authority, and through its leaders a shared sense of purpose, it does none of that any longer. Our faith in an open, inclusive and efficiently managed national polity has significantly diminished, and with it our trust has dissipated, not only in the structures of state upon which we depend, but also in those charged with managing those structures.

Australians' experience of the last couple of decades has been shaped by some deep-seated contradictions. On the one hand, cultural change has been wide-ranging and in some cases positively life-changing – think of same-sex marriage. Most would agree that there has been a marked increase in the diversity and density of everyday life in Australia; indeed, this has been described as the development of 'hyperdiversity'.[5] Much about our everyday lives has changed. Routine means of interpersonal communication that once were more or less universal – mail (that is, letters) and telephone calls – have been nudged aside by email, text messages and social media networks. The extent of our online engagement has dramatically expanded, extending from its initial institutional locations (school, the university or the workplace) into the heart of domestic life. We now increasingly go online to shop or to 'search' for recipes or lifestyle advice. Children and teenagers spend many hours a day on devices and using technologies that simply didn't exist when their parents were children.

For some, the nature of work has been revolutionised as well, with the promise of an entrepreneurial flexibility and independence generating a cultural shift that has created a largely unregulated gig economy. This shift was underpinned by American urban studies theorist Richard Florida's (now much questioned) celebration of 'creative' precarity.[6] Globalisation has opened up new domains of consumption, particularly in entertainment, travel and information, which have greatly expanded the menu of cultural choices open to us. In television alone, the last decade has seen Australia move from having a highly regulated broadcast and pay TV environment, with three national commercial networks and one major pay provider, to a position where the proliferating streaming services have become dominant. The market penetration of services such as Netflix has reached such a high level now that some industry observers question whether broadcast TV can survive in the future. Many of us who proudly built up a personal collection of the material objects onto which music is recorded (vinyl, tapes, CDs) are puzzled by a younger generation who don't buy music products at all but rather access them through their favourite playlists on Spotify and the like.

Developments such as these, one might think, should generate a sense of the culture opening up, of opportunities proliferating, of the available options outstripping the imagination. What is curious is that just such a sense of possibility actually coexists with what is also described above: a sense of the diminution of possibility, of things contracting. These two contradictory tendencies are not separate, however, but rather closely intertwined and interrelated – and they play out in ways that lead to complicated outcomes. For instance, the explosion in the provision of TV drama content to the Australian market due to the inroads of transnational streaming services such as Netflix has threatened the commercial support for locally produced drama. This is highly likely to have an impact on the number of Australian stories available to us in the future, unless there is some regulatory intervention. The success of music streaming services has expanded our access to the world of music but it has also wiped out the local CD store, and significantly affected the income of musicians as sales of CDs plummet and the financial returns from tracks played on streaming services are minimal.

Arguably, the pace of sociocultural change and its complicated outcomes are generating a weariness that feeds into a contrary tendency in some parts of the Australian electorate: that is, a reluctance to embrace, or even a fear of, significant political change.[7] I have encountered something like this over the last two decades in my work on the recent history of television. Those working in this area found that they needed to find a way to describe the audience's evident weariness with the multitude of options they had as video platforms proliferated. So screen studies theorist John Ellis coined the term 'choice fatigue'.[8] It is possible we are seeing something like change fatigue in our national culture, which has had to ride successive waves of significant change at the same time as it has endured a politics that has shown little interest in managing or understanding these changes in ways that might benefit the nation. The nation's citizens have largely been left to deal with it themselves.

Most recent academic research and debate about contemporary Australia, as well as most journalistic commentary and analysis, has focused on the roiling political landscape or upon debates about national economic policy. There has been less interest in analysing the significant changes within Australian culture and society that have occurred over this period. This book sets out to address key elements of this gap, and to demonstrate the usefulness of providing that kind of perspective on the contemporary moment. If Australians are indeed experiencing themselves as citizens of a shrinking nation – that is, if what now constitutes the nation in the public imagination has become diminished or compromised, or perhaps even fundamentally altered – then the details of such a reconstitution have serious implications not only for what Australia has become but also for what it might become in the future. We need to understand this better.

The chapters that follow address the state of the shrinking nation from a number of different perspectives. They look at the degraded state of Australia's political culture, the diminished capacities of government and our recent history of stalled progress and reform; they examine too the social consequences of the political dominance of neoliberal economics, and the cultural impact of the shifts in our information ecology created by the rise of digital and social media. At the level of policy formation, I explore the sidelining of the principle of the public good in public policy, and the effect of the 'culture wars' on some of our most significant cultural institutions, review some of the consequences of the business sector's capture of the idea of the national interest, and revisit the nation-building capacities of cultural policy. After discussing how social and cultural division has widened across so many of the fault lines within the national community, I consider how we might rebuild that community, making it more cohesive, inclusive, confident and resilient, while also renovating the manner in which it is served and protected by the state.

There is much that needs to be done to address the condition of the shrinking nation: a thorough renovation of the way we do politics, a reinvigoration of the political will to pursue progress and social justice, a revival of respect for expert advice and specialised knowledge, a reconsideration of what kind of country we wish to be and how that might be imagined, and a reinvestment in the state's responsibility to ensure the safety and wellbeing of all its citizens. As the last chapter argues, if we can turn our eyes away from the internal machinations of the political class and focus on the positive shifts within the wider culture, we might begin to see the signs of a better nation struggling to arise from the current malaise. The arguments and analyses presented in the following chapters are aimed at informing and assisting in that struggle.

CHAPTER 1

Diminished leaders, bad politics

'Pessimism about The State of Things recurs throughout history, and is rarely unique. But there seems something particularly rotten and fragile about our democracy right now – declining accountability, sharpening tribalism and an increasingly brazen skill to leverage the latter to conceal the former.'

Martin McKenzie-Murray[1]

Our starting point in developing these arguments and analyses is the dysfunctional state of Australia's political culture, and the reluctance within much of the political class to take on the responsibility of governing in the national interest. This has become a system captured by a self-interested and hyper-partisan politics, suffused with an arrogant disregard for maintaining appropriate levels of accountability in public life.

Concern about this situation built up considerably over the years of the Abbott/Turnbull/Morrison government.[2] That concern focused upon the partisan gridlocks blocking progress and reform, as well as on the debased quality of public debate on important political issues – what the political historian Judith Brett has described as the 'diminution of public life'.[3] The moments that have provoked such criticisms of this government are disturbingly numerous. They include the multiple instances of policy paralysis and partisan brinkmanship over climate change and energy policy; the continual resort to obfuscation, prevarication or just straight-out lies about government decisions, statements or policy settings; and the infuriating tactic (perfected by Morrison) of first denying the existence of a crisis, then seeking a means of deflecting attention from it or deferring action to deal with it, before finally buckling under pressure to do what is then regarded as too little, too late.

The public exasperation with the state of our political culture has been wearily channelled by journalists such as Laura Tingle, who famously wrote (in the *Australian Financial Review*, of all places) that we 'actually are being governed by idiots and fools'; in *The Sydney Morning Herald*, Ross Gittins mournfully hoped that maybe 'sometime, somewhere we [might find] leaders interested in doing a better job'.[4] The pandemic, of course, has provided the backdrop against which almost all of these behaviours have been on display, but the problems go back further in time. It has been incremental, this slow winding down of the Australian polity. While there are many markers along the way, there doesn't seem to be any one clear turning point. Judith Brett has wondered about this:

> When did it start, this sense that Australia has lost direction? In 1996, when Pauline Hanson brought her mean-spirited grievances into the national parliament? In 2001, when John Howard refused to let the captain of the *Tampa* land desperate refugees rescued from drowning? In 2008 and 2009, when Kevin Rudd was so intent on wedging Malcolm Turnbull that he destroyed the possibility of a bipartisan energy policy? Or was it the next year, when the ALP's bovver boys convinced Julia Gillard to challenge Rudd for the leadership; or 2013, when

Tony Abbott was elected on a series of lies about his plans for the budget, and became Australia's worst prime minister ever?[5]

Whenever it actually began, Australian politics itself has shrunk – not only in its substance and effect, but also because the public appears to have become resigned to the fact that participation in the world of policy and governance is now restricted to the professional politician. As politics has become more tribal, and loyalty to core ideologies becomes more important than rational consideration of action in the national interest, the world of politics and the world that the rest of us live in have become disconnected. Former Labor politician Lindsay Tanner raised this issue more than a decade ago, in his critical account of federal politics and its relation to the media:

> Our democratic process is at risk of returning to the patterns of the early nineteenth century, when very small elites totally dominated public decision-making. In those days, formal wealth, income, and status barriers excluded the mass of the population. Now, new barriers to participation built on ignorance and distraction are beginning to emerge.[6]

Today, it seems undeniable that the demographic pool from which our politicians are drawn has shrunk, and that the diversity of life experiences they bring into the parliament has steadily contracted over the years. There are strong similarities in the social backgrounds, cultural values and career paths of those (mostly, still, men) who make it into parliament. The emergence of the 'teal' independents has provided something of a corrective to this, at least in terms of gender – but notwithstanding their successes in 2022, it still makes clear sense to refer to something called 'the political class': a social grouping composed of those employed, according to Bernard Keane, in one 'of the range of occupations linked to political life' – political staffer, party executive, MP, lobbyist, consultant, media commentator and so on. As Keane describes it, this is a 'self-contained class that often appears uninterested in re-engaging the electorate, that appears focused on its own concerns rather than representing the concerns of voters'.[7]

If the sphere of influence of this political class has consolidated, however, the size of its popular base has shrunk. Membership of political parties has plunged from the heyday of the post-war years to the point where each of the two major parties are only attracting around 60,000 Australians, and the Nationals even fewer. (For comparison, Menzies' Liberal Party had a membership of 197,000 in the 1950s, drawn from a national population less than half the size it is today.) In 2020, less than 0.5 per cent of the Australian population was signed up to the mainstream political parties. In contrast, we see the rise of grassroots issue-based campaigns and independent candidates nominating for election in state and federal seats, and eventually taking votes away from both the major parties. The activist group GetUp claims to have more paid-up members than all the mainstream political parties put together.[8]

Political parties with such a narrow membership base face increasing difficulty in convincing us that they are representative of the broader community.[9] The disciplined uniformity of their candidates also leaves the public looking in vain for some kind of authenticity, a legible history of life experiences with which they might identify. The popular satirical segment presented for many years by John Clarke and Bryan Dawe at the end of ABC TV's *7.30* on Thursday nights saw Clarke playing a wide variety of politicians, without making any attempt to modify his appearance, voice or discourse. The implication was that there was no point in attempting any kind of impersonation, since they were all creatures of the same system: they were 'interchangeable'.[10]

In contrast to the products of these party machines, the independent senator Jacqui Lambie has earned respect across political lines precisely because she has remained true to what her life experiences tell her, and has maintained an authentic public presence (and, powerfully, her anger). Similarly, several of the senators 'accidentally' elected as a result of the preference deals that skewed the outcomes of the 2013 Senate election – notably Ricky Muir and Glenn Lazarus – turned out not to be the joke they were initially assumed to be. Their unapologetic ordinariness, their diligence and commitment to doing the job properly, as well as their principled decision-making, won them respect. Unfortunately, however, these are the exceptions; it is hard to come up with similar figures from within the major parties.

The public's disaffection with politics, and in turn our politicians' apparent disinterest in fulfilling their representative function, are exacerbated by a reconfiguration of the public sphere that has weakened the shared sense of a common culture. Social media, as its uses have evolved, has provided a base for both pro-social and antisocial activity. In regard to the latter, however, many platforms have effectively undermined the traditional role of the mainstream media as a universally available and generally accepted source of truth, blurring the lines between information and entertainment, and disrupting the conceptual distinction between fact and opinion. The public sphere today, while in many of its forms still striving to serve its traditional role as the fundamental ground for a civil democracy, also includes media platforms that have played, wittingly or not, quite different roles. They have fragmented communities, amplified false information and created closed information bubbles that are actively defined by their separation from, or their opposition to, a shared or common national culture.

All this is something of a perfect storm for civil society, coinciding not only with considerable social and cultural volatility but also with weak political leadership, compromised structures of governance and service delivery, and the absence of any sustained interest in progress and reform within the major parties.

The state of things

When I started work on this book in the last days of 2021, a string of media reports and commentary pieces were claiming that change was in the air, as dissatisfaction with the status quo in federal politics had intensified.[11] The provocation for these reports was a spike in the number of independent candidates in Liberal heartland electorates ahead of the 2022 federal election, and the mobilisation of the 'Voices of' movement, which focused on unseating incumbent Coalition MPs.

In another notable development around this time, former Liberal leader John Hewson and former ALP president Barry Jones joined forces to establish the Truth and Integrity Project, a social media–focused advocacy project targeting Prime Minister Scott Morrison's record on 'integrity matters and climate action'. *Guardian* journalist Katharine Murphy reported that Jones had come on board because he believed that democracy was under serious threat, and that neither the Coalition nor the federal ALP had any vision beyond the election of 2022.[12]

Criticism of the state of federal politics had arisen across the political spectrum, from business lobby groups as well as progressive and activist organisations, from peak bodies representing the full gamut of social services, from investment groups seeking firm policy settings for the future, from Indigenous leaders seeking to be heard at all, and from campaigners on domestic violence and gender equality. It peaked with the disruption of 'politics as usual' that occurred in the federal election in 2022. The results of that election, with the significant reduction in support for the major parties, provided clear proof that many Australians were dismayed by what their nation had become, by its failure to do better and by the politicians they had elected to represent them.

This point of view had, of course, been reinforced by the way many of Australia's politicians handled their responsibilities over the course of the pandemic. On the one hand, to be sure, there was the achievement of national unity generated by the national cabinet in 2020, and the strong leadership demonstrated by the state premiers over much of that year. On the other hand, once the immediate crisis appeared to have passed, that unity did not last. The federation disintegrated into states, regions and local government areas (LGAs). More significantly, the performance of the federal government and at least one state government over 2020 and 2021 drew accusations of incompetent governance and service delivery, fiscal irresponsibility, a lack of accountability and transparency, and even corruption.[13] Australians are entitled to be alarmed by their governments' long list of what many would see as policy failures over the last decade and a half. These include (and this is just an indicative list) failures on addressing climate change, on finding a humane resolution to the refugee situation, on managing the Covid-19 vaccines rollout, on making even minimal progress with Closing the Gap, and on properly responding to the broad-based societal and cultural concerns highlighted in the widespread criticism of government inaction over women's rights and safety.

As this last example suggests, these are not just issues of policy. They are also cultural, moral and ethical issues to do with the values and attitudes that have come to shape the culture of politics in Australia. The values implicit in the actions of both major political parties have been repeatedly questioned over the last decade or so. For example (and apologies for the long list, but that is part of the point), critics have targeted their disregard for human rights (asylum seekers on Nauru), their stubborn lack of compassion and perhaps even common sense (the needless saga over the Murugappan family, asylum seekers who hoped to settle in Biloela, Queensland), their callously punitive targeting of the most vulnerable (the Robodebt scandal), their reluctance to address entrenched sexism and misogyny in the federal parliament (the response to the 'Enough Is Enough' protests), their political cynicism in framing fraudulent campaign strategies ('Mediscare'), their incapacity for genuine empathy (the response to the Black Summer bushfires), their opportunistic dog-whistling on race (Muslims and national security), their lack of courage in policy positioning (fence-sitting on increasing the JobSeeker rate), and their endlessly flexible relationship with objective facts, or what the rest of us still describe as 'the truth' (just about every election campaign in recent memory).

Ancient as it is, the British political TV sitcom *Yes Minister* still has things to tell us about the sources of our disappointment. Sir Humphrey, the model of a kind of career public servant who probably no longer exists, is charged with educating his newly appointed minister, Jim Hacker, in the realities of government. Thrust into a ministerial role to which he appears to bring no relevant skills, interest or experience, Hacker wants to know why he was appointed. Sir Humphrey tells him that, rather than appointing people of 'genuine ability' to ministerial or leadership roles, political parties choose to appoint people who possess 'all kinds of other dazzling qualities – including enviable intellectual suppleness and moral manoeuvrability'. Unfortunately, in

Australia, we seem to have missed out on intellectual suppleness, but we have moral manoeuvrability in spades.

Big country, small leaders

Nowhere are our problems more apparent than in relation to our national leaders. For a start, it is striking that there have been so many. Between 2010 and 2018, four sitting prime ministers were removed by internal party coups – Rudd, Gillard, Abbott and Turnbull. To put that in some perspective, as politics professor Rodney Tiffen points out, over the preceding 100 years only three sitting prime ministers were the victims of party coups.[14] In none of the four cases since 2010 was the electorate directly involved, although shifts in public opinion polls were certainly prominent in the justifications offered by Gillard, Rudd (mark II) and Turnbull. The role of climate change policy (or the lack thereof) was crucial in various ways. The failure to address it convincingly proved critical for the two deposed Labor leaders, while the deep division within the Coalition parties over the science of climate change created a power base for Abbott, and became a political liability for Turnbull.

However, these leaders were not deposed just because of their failures of policy. The coups were all, in one way or another, the outcomes of factional deals, heightened electoral anxieties, deep personal animosities and the pursuit of personal ambition.[15] They were not demonstrations of the vitality of democracy. Rather, they were the result of what journalist and commentator Nick Bryant has described as the 'overpoliticisation' of politics.[16] This is the conduct of politics as a game in which access to power is the primary goal – perhaps even the only goal – while the use of that power to serve the national interest features only as a secondary consideration.

It is often suggested that leadership roles are something a person can 'grow into'. The idea is that taking on responsibility on behalf of others can bring out the best in a person, amplifying their capacity to think on behalf of the whole of their community or organisation, and to lead it towards achievement. Each of these disposable leaders, with the possible exception of Tony Abbott, came to power carrying considerable popular expectation that they might grow into the job. The result, unfortunately, in all of these cases, was that by the time they had lost their prime ministership they were much diminished figures. They shrank in the job.

Kevin Rudd initially enjoyed high levels of popularity (with the public, if not among his colleagues).[17] He recentred the nation's moral compass with the apology to the Stolen Generations, and his government's handling of the global financial crisis was decisive and effective. However, his failure to address what he called 'the great moral challenge of our generation' by effectively responding to climate change had a dramatic effect on his popularity and led to his replacement. In his case, though, it was not so much his failures in office that resulted in his personal diminution, but what Tiffen describes as his 'relentless, monomaniacal pursuit of revenge' on Julia Gillard and her supporters afterwards.[18]

For her part, Gillard enjoyed something of a honeymoon on taking office, and was highly successful in progressing legislation in a minority government. Under the pressures of leadership, however, Gillard appeared to lose touch with what had been a strong sense of her own authenticity and integrity, as she dutifully recited the party talking points ad nauseam. Even a promise to allow voters to see 'the real Julia' failed to arrest her slide in support, which had accelerated when she broke an election promise by introducing what Abbott successfully labelled a 'carbon tax'. Gillard became increasingly vulnerable to the continued attacks from a prowling Rudd, and a shameful barrage of misogyny from her opponents in parliament, as well as from sections of the media.[19] Unlike Rudd, however, she accepted her eventual defeat with great dignity and withdrew from the political sphere.

If it is possible to argue that Abbott grew into the job, it would not be in a good way. He became something of a monster once elected, ripping off the mask he had worn throughout the campaign to reveal the zealot beneath. Abbott had led Australian voters to hope he might be a more centrist leader in government than he had been in opposition ('no cuts to education, no cuts to healthcare, no cuts to the ABC', he had promised). Then came the infamous federal budget of 2014, and what commentator Tim Dunlop has described as 'the normalisation of bad politics'.[20] While some on the conservative fringe continue to sing his praises, most would agree with journalist Laura Tingle that the hyper-partisan Abbott turned out to be an 'utterly destructive force in Australian politics'.[21] By the end, he was so on the nose with the electorate that he not only lost the leadership of his party, but he also lost his own seat. He has continued to lurk, making occasional sorties into the public arena when opportunities arise, but the historical judgement on his leadership will not be positive.

Malcolm Turnbull, the urbane and moderate patrician, was a dramatic contrast to the pugnacious 'Mad Monk'. His ascent to the leadership of the Liberal Party was welcomed by many on both sides of politics – and there's the rub, of course, for some in the Liberal Party. There was reason to hope that he would take conservative politics back towards a more sensible centre and transform the schoolyard politics of Canberra into something closer to what he described as an 'adult conversation' rather than a fusillade of three-word slogans. The public enthusiasm was not replicated within his party, however, and over time the opinion polls revealed that the public eventually gave up on him. The adult conversation never eventuated. What we had instead was what the journalist and author David Marr memorably described as 'civilised blather' and, yes, three-word slogans ('Jobs and Growth'). As had been the case with Gillard, the compromises required to secure the leadership proved fatal. Hobbled by internal divisions, fenced in by the terms of the coalition between the Liberals and the National Party, and mercilessly targeted by the Murdoch press, Turnbull failed to take the positive policy initiatives so many had hoped he would, particularly on climate change.

Turnbull's successor, Scott Morrison, became personally central to public perceptions of the federal government's incompetence, secrecy and lack of accountability. Even though Morrison may not have generated much promise in the first place, with a 2019 election campaign that was almost entirely policy-free, he left office a much reduced figure.

Many saw this coming. According to *The Sydney Morning Herald*'s political columnist, Niki Savva, writing in 2021: 'As Scott Morrison approaches three years as Prime Minister, an achievement in its own right, it is also right that Australians consider whether over that time he has grown into his job or if he has shrivelled.' Savva claimed that it is 'fair enough to ask if Morrison has proved he is up to it, [and] whether he has the courage, the ability and the wisdom to see the country through these most testing times'. She went on to quote polling results that, she said, suggested Australians were questioning whether Morrison 'has the physical, intellectual or mental ability or even the empathy to lead, to earn trust, build coalitions, forge consensus, or to be something more than a moneybags, a punching bag or a spokesman for the premiers'.[22]

It is notable how similar the language was from other commentators at the time. Sarah Martin, *The Guardian*'s political correspondent, told us that 'when the country was looking desperately for some leadership, Scott Morrison shrank to the occasion'.[23] French president Emmanuel Macron's public accusation that Morrison had lied to him about their submarine contract gave a licence for widespread media commentary on Morrison's frequent troubles with the truth, further eroding the public's respect for his leadership. The 2022 election was very much driven by such concerns, and it delivered a resounding repudiation of Morrison's approach to politics. The revelations that continued to roll out in the succeeding months – the secret ministries, for instance – have only reconfirmed that repudiation.[24]

It is important to note how removed and disconnected much of this has been, the extent to which the Australian public has been held hostage to a parochial and personalised political game conducted at a distance from the concerns of the rest of the country. This is an issue raised by one of the independents elected in 2022 as a key reason for her decision to contest the election. When Allegra Spender, the daughter of fashion designer Carla Zampatti and former Liberal minister John Spender, announced her candidacy for the blue-ribbon Liberal seat of Wentworth, she pointed to the gulf of values and understanding between the government and the community. 'The disconnect is huge,' she said, 'between what decent people say is important to them and what they see playing out on the television in Canberra.'[25] In this observation, Spender was identifying what has arguably become, within Canberra, a diminished conception of the role of national politics and a blinkered disregard for the scale and significance of the issues at stake.

If our leaders have 'shrivelled', to use Niki Savva's term, Australia has shrunk along with them. The legitimacy and capacity of the Commonwealth government has diminished, with the accompanying public frustration at a gridlocked and hyper-partisan political sphere and its paralysing consequences for the development of policy, the provision of information to the public and the quality of public debate. While this public frustration eventually led to a change of government, with promises to inaugurate a better political culture, the malaise has been decades in the making. Even with the best of intentions – and some of these are beginning to materialise – it will take time to restore what has been lost.

Some things the pandemic taught us

If they hadn't been quite so apparent previously, the pandemic has certainly exposed the fault lines that already compromised our institutional and government structures, especially in relation to our stewardship of those structures which are meant to protect the national wellbeing. Some of the core beliefs of a neoliberal politics, in particular, took a beating as Australia saw the practical outcomes of the ideological pursuit of small government and market fundamentalism. The limitations to what Australian governments could effectively do to protect their citizens were dramatically revealed. These ranged from the market's damaging failure to provide sufficient supplies of personal protective equipment (PPE) for health workers to the complex and dysfunctional patchwork of state and federal responsibilities for hospitals, public health, quarantine and border protection – not to mention the occasionally disastrous consequences of outsourcing key elements of this patchwork (such as hotel quarantine) to private providers. The pandemic exposed the human cost of years of underinvestment in public healthcare and the consequences of privatising community services that are as fundamental to national health and wellbeing as aged care and childcare.

Among the developments with the most long-term implications was the demonstration of how whole sectors of the economy (retail, agriculture, transport, hospitality) were dependent upon the supply of low-paid casual workers largely provided through immigration and a steady flow of backpackers and international students. Workers in these industries, while essential to the continued functioning of society, also turned out to be among those least able to protect themselves from the virus because they did not have the white-collar luxury of working from home. There was therefore a class basis to this, which linked the curve of the virus to existing patterns of inequality.

And then there was the temporary increase in the JobSeeker payment (as well as its extension to those not so easily characterised as undeserving), which, paradoxically, served to highlight the hardships inevitably created by an unnecessarily punitive welfare system that justified itself by stigmatising its recipients. We had been warned earlier on, of course, and repeatedly, about such things, most vividly by journalist and writer Bernard Keane in his polemical account of how 'a civilisation has lost its way', in *The Mess We're In: How politics went to hell and dragged us with it.* However, it seemed we had to live through the consequences of 'the mess we're in' before we fully understood the potentially disastrous ramifications.

Over 2021 and 2022, one of the key concerns involved the depleted state of health services outside the state capitals. The difficulties experienced in delivering Covid-19 vaccines into the regions, and the likely consequences of an outbreak in sizeable country towns that perhaps only had one intensive-care bed in their hospital, made it clear that the coronavirus pandemic presented an even more worrying threat to rural residents than it did to those in the cities. Until then, the issue of emergency preparedness in the regions was rarely discussed in the metropolitan press, unless some kind of natural disaster occurred – floods, fires or drought. Covid was even more notable than these, in its way, as it highlighted the social and economic cost of the structural disparity between the level of services available in regional areas and in the cities, and the degree to which the political focus – both among politicians and in the political media – had been routinely on urban areas rather than the country.[26]

None of these fault lines is new. Their existence and projected consequences have been raised repeatedly with governments over the years, and they come up regularly within media commentary. However, in a depressing pattern that affects more than just these issues, the voices that speak most directly from a concerned community tend to be those which are most likely to be treated as 'special interests' or 'rent seekers'. This points to another tendency that Covid-19 has exposed – ironically, by the fact that the pandemic has necessitated a temporary shift in attitude. This is the entrenched political disdain for mid-term to long-term expert and evidence-based foresighting advice on policy. The 'campaign against established knowledge' that Tom Nichols' *The Death of Expertise* has examined in the United States has parallels here. We may not have yet reached the point he describes – 'where ignorance, especially of anything related to public policy, is an actual virtue'[27] – but there are those who might take us there, such as certain populist talk radio hosts, or the pack of political pundits howling at the moon on Sky News After Dark, or the hardcore neoliberals spitting fury in the opinion pages of *The Australian*.

Where scientists, academics, members of the judiciary, clerics, union leaders, educators or other respected community figures might once have been considered among the legitimate participants in any broad-based public policy debate, this has largely changed.[28] The media tend to ignore them, and the politicians do too. A key issue motivating the teal independents was their perception that Australian politics had contracted into a game played only by career politicians – who then police any incursion into their territory by attacking the messenger rather than by engaging with their point of view or their suggestions (something that was perfectly demonstrated, in fact, by the way the major parties then dealt with the emergence of the teals).

To do this, the members of the old guard manipulate information in such a way as to undermine the authority of their critics or misrepresent their views; they incite fear, anger or, at worst, hatred in order to discredit their opponents or their views; they deploy divisive labels such as 'cultural elites' to delegitimise and separate the objectors from 'the rest of us'; they make the slightly desperate accusation that these folks are 'just playing politics' (unlike the politicians!); and, when all else fails, they revert to straight-out schoolyard name-calling.

Bad politics

The authority of those with knowledge and expertise has become one of the casualties of the contemporary practice of politics in Australia. We are one of several Western democracies in which an emerging fraction of the political culture has invented its own realities, its 'alternative facts', which generally have only a distant connection to actual evidence. Over time, we have also seen conservative parties, in particular, become excessively tribal in their beliefs, increasingly choosing to generate fear and anger within the electorate as a means of holding onto their so-called electoral base.

Early instances of this, while John Howard was prime minister, include the ramping-up of the *Tampa* crisis, the deliberate circulation of misinformation during the 'Children Overboard' affair, and the cynical exploitation of the xenophobia and Islamophobia released by the 'War on Terror' after the attacks of 11 September 2001. However, it was when Tony Abbott took the leadership of the federal opposition that this new order really fell into place, and began shaping the culture of 'bad politics' Australia has been stuck with ever since.[29]

Abbott adopted the same tactic in opposition that Republican speaker of the House of Representatives Newt Gingrich had used against the Democratic administration of President Bill Clinton in the United States during the 1990s, opposing absolutely everything the administration proposed, irrespective of merit. For Abbott, the goal was to destroy Labor by making it impossible for them to govern. This single-minded focus on securing power changed the culture of politics within Canberra, and ultimately within the electorate too.

This was a politics based upon the creation of stark and irreconcilable division, and that fundamentally denied the legitimacy of any competing points of view. It was propagated with half-truths, endlessly repeated slogans and stuff that politicians just made up. The result is the excessive partisanship we experience today. It seems as if there can no longer be sensible conversations between different points of view within Australian federal politics. Policy is now hopelessly enmeshed within a shark net of fixed political positions, with no room for compromise or collaboration, no matter what the cost to the nation.

Abbott's revolution created a national polity that was poorly equipped to deal with a crisis such as the global pandemic. Pollster Peter Lewis has identified specific issues related to the contemporary conduct of politics, pointing to the decline of trust in the authority of individual leaders, the collapse of the media as a single point of truth, and the hollowing-out of public services.[30] The role of the media in all of this certainly does demand examination. This is particularly due to the ways in which the reconfiguration of the public sphere, and in particular the rise of social media, has undermined and fragmented not only trust and authority but also the modes of community that are so essential to the idea and the experience of belonging to the nation.

The potential consequences of this are disturbing. We have the dystopian example of Trump's America, where large sections of the population accept the dangerous misinformation fed to them on social media and cable TV, where agreement on even the most basic of facts is now apparently impossible. The Australian media's failure to call out similar tendencies within our politics and the increasing circulation of unregulated misinformation to the public have already caused damage here – such as the rise of unfounded conspiracy theories within the anti-vaxxer movement, the physical attacks upon health workers in vaccination clinics, and the heightened incidence of threats of violence from protesters against lockdowns and vaccine mandates in Victoria.

Finally, there is one crucial aspect of this political culture which has deep roots in our history and has become particularly prominent in recent years. This is the way in which political conversations have effectively reduced the concept of the nation to the functioning of the economy, and from that to the interests of the business sector. Because of this narrowing-down of what now constitutes the nation, the interests of society, culture, national wellbeing, heritage and, most substantively, the public good have been sidelined. We are now living with the consequences of that in all kinds of ways. Service to the public good needs to be put back in the picture – it must again become fundamental to what we as a nation require from our politicians.

Hope and change

In February 2010, speaking at the first national Tea Party convention in the United States, former vice presidential candidate Sarah Palin spent much of her time mocking the achievements of the 'Yes, we can' president, Barack Obama, who had been inaugurated a little more than a year earlier. Elected on a wave of enthusiasm for a new kind of American politics, Obama hit trouble once he was forced to deal with a Congress dominated by representatives who relished the opportunity of saying 'No, you can't' to every one of his initiatives. Palin's speech focused on the administration's performance on the economy and national security, before taunting its supporters by asking the crowd: 'How's that hopey-changey thing workin' out for ya?' It was a telling line. Even Obama's supporters would have acknowledged their disappointment over what had been achieved so far. For the Tea Party faithful, the taunt tapped into the frustration and disillusionment with 'politics as usual' that would eventually lead to Trump's election six years later.

Australia had its own 'hopey-changey thing' when Kevin Rudd was elected in 2007 on a wave of enthusiasm for something like that. The hope it generated didn't last – although for different reasons to those affecting Obama's period in office. The consequences have nevertheless been similar.

Faced with what is now a political culture so polarised that it is prepared even to make government fail, the electorate has lost trust in the political system and become wary of hoping for better. For their part, politicians from both major parties have become leery of promising anything: they become particularly skittish when faced with any proposal for change that might have negative effects on those they think of as part of their electoral base. Since most proposals of any substance are bound to have negative consequences for somebody – and particularly for those most likely to be benefiting from the status quo – change itself has become a thing to be avoided. Ahead of the 2022 federal election, the lack of strong policy proposals from either major party prompted *Guardian* journalist Sarah Martin to describe the impending contest as looking like a 'nothing-off'.[31]

The outcome of that election may, however, hold out some hope for change in the practice of politics into the future. The busy manner in which the current government has taken to its task once elected does suggest there is ambition on some crucial policy fronts. Federal treasurer Jim Chalmers' suggestion that the nation's 'wellbeing', and not just the nation's economy, will be of interest to the current government has been welcomed by many and does signal a significant shift in focus.[32] However, it is clear that bold reforms remain unlikely, and our political culture too is so far largely unchanged. As a result, there is a danger that Australian politics will continue to be stuck in a defensive stance that recoils at the prospect of significant shifts in position. Given the world we live in now, with the proliferation of looming challenges to which we must find ways to adapt, such a stance severely limits what Australia can do that might help its people take better control of their futures.

While sociocultural change has already transformed what it feels like to live in contemporary Australia, institutional politics has too often lagged behind these changes, or actively frustrated them. Over the last decade, it has become abundantly clear that this kind of politics has not been good enough – and it certainly won't be good enough in the future.

CHAPTER 2

How good's the status quo?

The last two decades have been shaped by successive waves of significant change – technological, social and cultural. The rise of digital media, the adoption of mobile devices, the migration of automation from the factory floor to the algorithms of social media, and the increasing application of artificial intelligence across the public and private sectors all have profound implications for Australia's economy, society and culture.

While major improvements in convenience, connectedness and mobility have all flowed from these developments, it is also the case that these advances in technology have occurred at a pace that has outstripped the capacity of the community to fully understand and manage them in their own interests. Regulatory structures designed for the nation's mass media, for instance, are not at all suited to social media platforms or video streaming services. Updating them has proved to be an extremely difficult task, both practically and politically.

More importantly perhaps – and notwithstanding the early optimism about the democratising potential of the digital revolution – control of how these technologies work, and in whose interests, has become highly concentrated in the hands of the global technology giants: Google, Meta (Facebook), Amazon and Apple. A great many concerns have been raised about precisely how these giants of Big Tech use their commercial, social and cultural power. The global scale of their dominance is unprecedented, and so their development presents significant problems for national governments to address within their own jurisdictions, while also revealing governments' limited power to negotiate what are ultimately issues of national sovereignty.

Many of the most significant social changes to have occurred over this period are reflected in the indicators of rising inequality in Australia. Not only has there been stubborn political resistance to improving the lot of the unemployed, but there is now also an underclass of employees working in the 'gig economy', with unregulated hours, rates of pay that ignore award wages, and limited or no entitlements to sick leave or other benefits. These gig workers have also been subjected to what seems almost systemic wage theft across a range of industries, from hospitality, retail and agriculture to higher education.

Our daily news feeds have been keeping us all in touch, incessantly, with what is the most important factor in all of this: the redistribution of wealth caused by the dramatic rise in housing values. This has greatly increased the wealth of some property owners – who are mostly older – while shutting out others – generally younger people – from the housing market altogether. The wealth that home ownership generates has benefited the top 20 per cent of the population, and the spread of home ownership has contracted accordingly. According to an Australian Council of Social Service (ACOSS) report, the wealth of this group has grown by 68 per cent over the past fifteen years, compared to a 6 per cent increase for the bottom 20 per cent.[1]

Researchers from the Grattan Institute have found that between 1981 and 2016, the proportion of home owners among the poorest 20 per cent of Australian households had fallen from 63 per cent to 23 per cent.[2] Young people are bearing a disproportionate amount of the burden of this. Over the same period, the percentage of those with a mortgage in the age group 25–34 had fallen from 60 per cent to 45 per cent.[3] Combine that with this cohort's heightened exposure to the precarity of casual employment contracts, the debts incurred as a result of their education and their particular vulnerability to the looming consequences of the global failure to address climate change, and one can see why Bernard Keane might suggest that Australia is waging 'a war on the young'.[4]

The expanding use of digital media has also been among the primary drivers of cultural change during this time, and their points of intervention into our everyday lives have increased. As Australians become more connected to their mobile devices, they have changed how they access their workplaces, search for information, consume entertainment, do their shopping and connect with each other. The now ubiquitous 'culture of search' – 'googling it' – is changing how we think and know, and has effectively extended our information and entertainment horizons beyond the local and the national to the global. Smartphones and tablets have changed what counts as normal personal behaviour in the home, in the workplace and in public – and there are complex patterns of differences which determine how this plays out across generations, genders, ethnicities and social class.[5] For many, the experience of work changed during the Covid-19 pandemic lockdowns, with virtual workplaces providing the increased flexibility that lockdowns demanded and ushering in what may well be permanent shifts in the relations between work and home.

The construction of shared communities is changing as well, as online engagement dramatically affects the character of Australians' participation in their culture. The online environment, however, is an unruly and lawless cultural space, with as much potential to create division and disruption as to build connections. And, indeed, cultural division, actively fomented by more than two decades of culture wars, is among the key characteristics of our history in recent years. Fault lines have opened up between generations, genders and sociocultural identities.

While Australia's cultural diversity is gradually becoming more visible in our media, and indeed in our federal parliament, there remains a residual reservoir of racism which can resurface under pressure – in the discriminatory regulatory regimes established within some communities in Melbourne and Sydney during the Covid lockdowns, for instance. The passing of the same-sex marriage bill may have reflected a growing tolerance of sexual difference and the fluidity of gender identities, but that did not prevent the Coalition from using the confected issue of transgender athletes in an attempt to energise its base during the 2022 federal election campaign. Finally – underlying and feeding into all of this – there is a sociocultural tendency that is becoming increasingly significant: the weakening of the national imagining of a shared, common culture.

While these and other changes have swept across the nation over the last two decades, our politics have seemed stuck, frozen in a posture of defence and denial. Meanwhile, the list of pressing policy challenges and social issues now demanding urgent attention from a new federal government has continued to grow. To name just some (and this is another long list, I'm afraid, but again that is the point), there have been widespread public calls for proper policy development aimed at addressing the roiling crises across the caring professions (aged care, childcare, hospitals); providing more comprehensive and appropriate support for those with disabilities and mental health conditions; exploring serious solutions to the housing crisis and the increase in homelessness; properly regulating the gig economy and reining in exploitative patterns of employment; taking action on the full list of recommendations presented in the *Respect@Work* report on sexual harassment in the workplace; establishing a federal integrity commission with real teeth to combat misconduct and corruption in public office; resolving the standoff over the establishment of an Indigenous Voice to Parliament; and finally acting on the widespread public perception that there is a need to increase the rate of JobSeeker benefits, which for so long has punished and stigmatised the unemployed. That's a great many important issues, and not one of them is niche. All have generated broad and sustained public concern across the community and across political lines for years – in some cases, for decades.

To be sure, some of these issues are being taken up by the new federal Labor government and by a number of state governments, although progress remains slow. Regrettably, however, the formal political response on so many of them, from both major parties, continues to be characterised by denial, delay, deflection, personal attacks on those advocating change, and spin and misinformation. Across the whole of the political class, there is a dogged, almost irrational, defence of the status quo.

This was a prominent feature of the Coalition government led by Scott Morrison. Political commentator Sean Kelly claims that while Morrison himself may have said 'contradictory things' from time to time, his consistent pitch during the 2019 election was that 'he was the man for the status quo', an 'ordinary Australian who was immensely proud of Australia exactly as it was'. In 2021, furthermore, as Morrison foreshadowed how we might emerge from the pandemic, Kelly writes, Morrison promised 'a return to the status quo', 'to the way things were', acting as if 'the last two years didn't happen'.[6] *The Sydney Morning Herald*'s economics columnist Ross Gittins also noted at the time that Morrison showed little interest in any kind of reform, 'whether to advance business interests or anyone else. Reform involves persuading people to accept changes they don't like the sound of,' Gittins observed, 'and increases the risk they'll vote against you at the next election.'[7]

Indeed, the fear of advocating progressive reform has become entrenched among politicians of both colours, as they have come to believe that proposals for significant change will inevitably result in electoral defeat for their party. That conviction has been reinforced by the pressure placed upon politicians by a predominantly conservative and at times vigorously partisan press (the influence of Rupert Murdoch can't be ignored here), and by the massive expansion in the activity and influence of social media. The contemporary media-sphere, across both traditional and digital platforms, is now driven disproportionately by stories and opinion pieces that aim to generate fear and/or anger. These reactions are easily aroused but not so easily defused, we are now discovering, and their default political function is to stand in the way of change. A media landscape saturated with 'alternative facts', along with a proliferation of sites and platforms and the subsequent fragmentation of the audience, has radically increased the degree of difficulty for publicly engaging in anything like civilised, evidence-based political debate.

Ironically, and reflecting the diminished ambitions of the politics of the time, the Morrison government tried in its dying days to spin 'doing nothing' into something like a virtue rather than a mark of failure. However, their pitch for government to 'get out of the way' and let 'can-do capitalism' lead us out of trouble over the post-pandemic period generated immediate scepticism among media commentators. Amy Remeikis described it as a form of 'do nothing leadership', while Niki Savva characterised it as a 'subliminal pitch to fatigued voters': 'elect me and I will do nothing'.[8] Sean Kelly suggested that voters, no matter how fatigued, might still resist such a pitch to reaffirm the ideology of small government. On the one hand, he said, the pandemic showed us the ways that the government had failed us, 'largely through inaction: a failure to respond to a changing society, to recognise the inequities that were becoming greater issues'. On the other hand, it showed us, too, 'that governments that act can save lives. We might be sick of being told what to do, but most of us know that governments saved us, too.'[9] In the 2022 elections, voters made it clear that they wanted their governments to actually do things.

There had been some earlier, contrary indications that it was not only possible but advantageous for politicians to offer a reform agenda. In what the Australia Institute's economics commentator Richard Denniss described as a 'complete repudiation of the "neoliberal common sense" that has long dominated Australian politics', Daniel Andrews' 2018 campaign during the Victorian state election promised to 'spend big on services and infrastructure, invest heavily in skills and education and fund large one-off investments by increasing public debt'.[10] Not only was he elected, but he then proceeded to do what he said he would do (itself something of a novelty). The ambition of that strategy was an outlier, however, and it is notable that it provoked an unstinting campaign of vilification against 'Dictator Dan' from conservative politicians, Sky News commentators and the Murdoch press during the pandemic. Later, when the Murdoch press in Victoria launched a similarly bizarre scaremongering campaign against Andrews during the state election of 2022, voters again resisted. Federally, it now seems that the failure of Morrison's 'do nothing' agenda has actually encouraged the Labor government to harbour some ambition to deliver progressive reforms over its term in power.

It's an obvious point to make, perhaps, but we need to remember that it hasn't always been this way. The National Museum of Australia's online exhibition *Glorious Days: Social laboratory* introduces itself by pointing to a very different past:

> In 1913, Australia enjoyed an international reputation as the social laboratory of the world. Relatively free of the entrenched class divisions of the 'old world' and richly endowed with land and mineral resources, Australia's population of 'transplanted Britons' lived in a democracy with progressive social policies. To many, the country offered 'infinite potential' for the improvement of the race. Scientific research and new technologies transformed approaches to health, housing and nutrition. Traditionally disadvantaged groups looked for opportunities to shape the conditions of their lives. Women seized the vote in federal elections in Australia from 1902, and turned their attention to international suffrage and improving conditions for women to work and raise children. Trade unions sought to establish fairer conditions for workers.[11]

Our histories tell us that Australia was a world leader in progressive democratic reform in the nineteenth century, introducing universal male suffrage, secret ballots and the eight-hour working day.[12] Over most of the twentieth century, too, the Australian state was relatively interventionist, playing a fundamental role in the development of Australian society, with governing bodies always taking the lead in providing the infrastructure necessary for society to develop. According to historian Anthony Moran, our federal government over this period was explicitly 'nation-building', subsidising and supporting rural areas, setting up public housing schemes and so on.[13]

There were other periods of progressive reform later in the twentieth century as well. Nick Bryant writes of the 'great reform era, ushered in by Gough Whitlam's election in 1972 and accelerated in the 1980s and 1990s'. It was, he says, 'marked by bold initiatives that required political bravery and public elucidation, whether it was John Howard's unpopular decision to introduce the GST, Malcolm Fraser's open door policy towards the Vietnamese boat people, Bob Hawke's end of protectionism or Paul Keating's superannuation reforms'.[14]

George Megalogenis takes a similar view, although he selects slightly different moments, seeking periods in our history that 'genuinely combined policy innovation, political stability and a shared sense of purpose across the parties of labour and capital'. He nominates two periods in particular: the Curtin/Chifley/Menzies era between 1941 and 1966, and the Hawke/Keating/Howard era between 1983 and 2007. This selection exemplifies Megalogenis's focus on times when there was 'not always agreement on policy detail' but 'the nature of the problem was understood by both sides'.

By 2015, Megalogenis concludes, things were very different. The 'shared mission' was nowhere to be seen and 'neither party wants to concede even the smallest human error for fear of losing that minute's news cycle. If one side nominates an issue, the other feels compelled to deny its importance.'[15]

As Nick Bryant also notes, contemporary debates about policy tend not to be about determining action towards an outcome that reflects a shared view of the problem or of the national interest. Rather, he says, in the current climate, 'policy typically involves a political fix'.[16] Actually solving the problem is no longer the issue; managing the politics is what matters.

As Richard Denniss reminds us, then, 'the past is another country'. Australia is now a very different kind of social laboratory to what it was in 1913 – and not at all in a good way:

> Australians now work some of the longest hours in the developed world, unpaid overtime is the norm for most workers, and our unemployment benefits are among the stingiest in the developed world. Citizens are encouraged to dob in dole bludgers and keep an eye on suspect (Muslim) neighbours. Conservative politicians tell those who disagree with their worldview to leave our country. Yet although those same politicians have worked to undermine the collectivist spirit of our labour market and welfare system, they still talk endlessly about mateship and the Anzac spirit.[17]

This is a shift in our political culture so dramatic that it must make us wonder what has driven it. What does Australians' apparent acceptance of their politicians' resistance to change tell us about the culture, its declining trust and confidence in politics and democracy, the varying intensity of its identification with the national interest, and precisely how that national interest is conceptualised in the public's mind?

While much of the debate over such issues in recent years has focused upon the weakness of Scott Morrison's leadership, this is not a matter of personal pathologies. The tendencies extend across decades and party lines. Neither, in my view, is it only a matter of our politicians 'forgetting how to govern', as Laura Tingle has argued, although that idea has merit. There is also something in the suggestion that this generation of conservative politicians has so thoroughly internalised the neoliberal ideology of small government and market fundamentalism that, despite much evidence to the contrary, they may actually believe that the market can be relied on to do on its own all that is needed. The more depressing possibility, however, is not that this generation of politicians has actually forgotten how to govern or that they have become captive to their strict articles of political faith. Rather, it may be that they are simply not interested.

Political power? Absolutely. Governing … not so much

Over the last decade or so, and most consistently since the coup against Kevin Rudd's prime ministership, it has been widely argued that politics in Australia has been effectively repurposed. According to this analysis, the practice of politics in this country is now reducible to whatever it takes to gain or retain power. Those who have held that power appear much less bothered about what might be done in the national interest than was the case in the past. Furthermore, effectively managing the work of government – planning for the future, sourcing expert advice, developing and implementing policy, and efficiently delivering services – seems beyond this current generation of politicians. What's more – and even though it looks likely that the Albanese government may break with this pattern in time – most of our governments have seemed uninterested in learning how to do any of this better. Even when there has been a palpable failure of government administration (the vaccine rollout, for instance, or the debacle of rapid antigen Covid-19 test supplies), there is rarely an explicit commitment to explore ways of doing a better job. Bernard Keane has lamented that 'the most basic tasks of public life – doing the admin properly, delivering policy while remaining unified and keeping the confidence of the electorate – suddenly seem beyond politicians'.[18]

It is striking that even while there is so much public discussion about the incompetence of our governments, the political class remains largely unmoved. While they do offer the standard platitudes when challenged, asking for forbearance as they do their best to govern in the public interest, a critical reading of their actions tells a different story. 'Bizarre as it seems,' writes political science professor Keith Dowding, 'government no longer appears to see its role as looking after the welfare of its people.'[19] Although federal treasurer Jim Chalmers described his October 2022 budget as a 'wellbeing budget', to date not much of substance has been provided. Unfortunately, it appears, many Australians must face the fact that their wellbeing is just not their government's primary concern.

Laura Tingle provides some insight into the contextual factors helping to drive this situation when she points to how 'perpetual campaigning' – that is, the need to be continually responding to the accelerated news cycle – has 'changed the day-to-day workload and focus of our leaders'. This, she says, 'inevitably means the conversation is about political success', with the result that the 'value of governing inevitably diminishes'.[20]

Worse still, the administrative tools of government have been appropriated to serve party-political objectives; this was evident especially (but not exclusively) during the Abbott/Turnbull/Morrison era. The brutal reality of what our politics became during this period has been succinctly characterised by Wayne Errington and Peter van Onselen as 'rewarding friends and punishing enemies'.[21] An example of 'rewarding friends' was the funnelling of sports grants and car park development programs overwhelmingly to Coalition-held seats.[22] 'Punishing enemies' included the establishment of an automated debt-recovery strategy targeting Australia's most disadvantaged people in the unlawful Robodebt. At a broader level, prominent friends included the resources and fossil fuel industries, while the enemies included the public universities – hence their exclusion from the JobKeeper income-support program during the Covid-19 lockdowns.[23]

Errington and Van Onselen argue that this repurposing of politics, with its reliance on 'mates and corporate chequebooks' has meant that 'Australians put up with third-best policy outcomes due to a web of relationships, donations, favours, staff turnover between lobbying and government, and incumbent mediocrity across all sectors of the economy'.[24] Indeed, these 'friends' have shaped the political agenda: as Ross Gittins notes, the idea that the economy needs to be 'reformed' has been 'hijacked by the business lobby groups. Their notion of reform involves making life better for their clients at the expense of someone else.'[25]

Readers will have noticed how much of the foregoing refers to the performance of the Morrison government, and there is good reason for that. Many would regard Morrison and his cabinet as the nadir of a long-term process that has transformed the culture of politics in Australia over the last decade and a half. Their history of political indifference and administrative neglect – the true scale of which only fully emerged in the months after their departure from the Treasury benches – constitutes the shrinkage of the national project writ large. Morrison's performance of politics and his approach to government – bluntly, his treatment of both as a 'game' (the title of Sean Kelly's 2021 book about Morrison) – is the perfect manifestation of the parlous condition in which the nation finds itself.

David McKnight has argued that this condition is now systemic: that contemporary governments and the political parties that form them are simply no longer capable of focusing on the long term. Rather, the governments we have today are attuned to interest group pressure and represent an establishment of existing players, not future generations. Consequently, they operate in the short term, countenancing only small or incremental changes, and dismiss any call to address emerging crises as 'alarmism'.[26]

This analysis suggests that the shrinking nation is a consequence of what have become more or less permanent structural features of the culture of politics in contemporary Australia. While I question just how permanent they are, there certainly are structural factors which have influenced how this has come about. Two in particular have been major contributors to the rising primacy of the 'political fix': these are the politicisation and hollowing-out of the public service, and the increasing number and influence of political advisers.

Since the Howard government's period in office, the independence and expertise of the public service has been under attack. The changes in career paths for public servants, the importation of leaders from the private sector, and the running-down of portfolio-specific knowledge and expertise have weakened the public service as a source of policy advice and administrative know-how. Political historian Chris Wallace describes the Australian Public Service (APS) as being leaned on, undermined, underfunded and 'sidelined by private sector consultants [who have been] paid multiples of what equivalent – and often better – APS advice would have cost'.[27]

Rod Tiffen, among many others,[28] has claimed that the running-down of the public service has resulted in a significant reduction in the capabilities of government over this period:

> A couple of generations ago, the public service often had close to a monopoly of expertise in many policy areas. Now, internal weakening and the strengthening of external resources means that this is far from true. In the departments that deliver services and regulate areas of policy, there has been much higher turnover of

staff, and some areas have been outsourced to private contractors, resulting in reduced institutional memory.[29]

There may be some chance of this being turned around. Albanese has made a point of calling for a return to a 'strong and independent public service', reining in the private consulting industry, and reviving the proposals made by David Thodey's 2019 Independent Review of the Australian Public Service, which had been commissioned by Turnbull when he was prime minister, but mothballed since.[30] Positive signs, but the reversal of several decades of institutional attrition will require a major change in the culture not only of politics but of the whole of government, meaning any improvement will take a considerable amount of time.

The second factor – also widely noted by political commentators – is the increase in the number and the influence of political advisers. This is among the issues considered in the Grattan Institute's wide-ranging 2021 report on the 'gridlock' around policy reform in government. Researcher John Daley surveyed a range of 'blockages' to the processes of responsible and accountable government, and his report documents, among other things, the diminishing power of the public service and a corresponding increase in the power of the ministerial adviser. The number of these advisers has more than doubled in the last four decades, from 210 in 1983 to a total of around 450 today.[31] As many of us who have served as independent advisers to federal government departments over these years could attest,[32] the power of the political adviser has reached the point where they effectively constitute something like a parallel bureaucracy, competing with and, when necessary, overriding the advice of the public servants in their portfolio.

The competition between these two sources of advice is built into the system, as each of these components of government has very different objectives for their policy choices. Daley finds that the political advisers are likely to discourage ministers from 'pursuing an unpopular policy', since these advisers 'tend to be focused on winning the immediate war of public opinion in a culture of continuous campaigning'. Their job is to keep the minister out of political trouble rather than to pursue good policy. By contrast, Daley goes on, 'senior public servants are less worried about public opinion if they think the reform is in the public interest'.[33] The influence of the political adviser, then, is to do with politics rather than policy. Importantly, political advisers have direct access to their minister: they are usually located in the same office within Parliament House. Public servants, meanwhile, are housed in their department offices well away from Parliament House.

The background these advisers bring to their task has changed as well. During the Hawke/Keating period, many advisers were seconded from the public service, bringing with them years of experience and expertise in the design and implementation of policy. This, Daley suggests, was a key factor which enabled that government to 'pursue so much productive reform'. However, 'an increasing number of ministerial staffers today have strong party affiliations, little if any experience in the public service, often little experience beyond student politics, and aspirations either for pre-selection or a career in various forms of government advocacy'.[34] Most worryingly, however, ministerial staffers remain relatively unaccountable. Their names are not made public, and by convention they cannot be called to appear before parliamentary committees, whereas public servants can be. It is easy to see how this enhances their capacity to protect their minister and their party rather than being bound by any responsibility towards either the parliament or the public interest.

There have been repeated calls for the defects in this

arrangement to be remedied. These have included proposals for a cap on the number of advisers, for an enforceable code of conduct which might address some of the concerns about accountability, and for a quota mandating that at least half of all advisers have public service experience as a means of redressing the prioritising of politics over governing. Notwithstanding such proposals, Daley observes, it is unfortunately the case that 'for more than 30 years, governments have not shown any interest in restraining the growth and politicisation of ministerial advisers with little accountability'.[35]

As noted earlier, while the Coalition government resisted the wider set of recommendations for the reform of the public service advanced by the Thodey review in 2019,[36] these have attracted the interest of the current Labor government and look likely to be revisited during its first term. It is unlikely, however, that the role of the ministerial adviser will be more tightly regulated in the future.

Slogans rule

To our great national cost (and, most likely, our continuing personal frustration), the quality of political debate in Australia is at an all-time low. Complicated policy issues are reduced to slogans, which often bear no relation to any evidence, and which are actively designed to misrepresent and mislead. Close and informed analysis of policy detail has become less common in most of the traditional electronic and print media coverage of politics, effectively vacating the field to the circulation of misinformation or smear campaigns, and the mobilisation of fear and resentment.

Much of this is done at the level of language, through the very terms in which the political culture articulates itself. Increasingly, that is through the repeated use of name-calling and slogans which simplify division and disable debate by sidestepping the necessity for the consideration of evidence or other points of view. When repeated often enough, they can seem as though they refer to something that actually exists – we see this in the effectiveness of labels such as 'cultural elites', 'debt and deficit disaster' or 'carbon tax', for example. The political contest is transformed into a crudely articulated culture war that pits one bunch of labels – that is, one set of unsubstantiated accusations – against another. The point is to weaponise the divisions the culture war has helped to create in order to secure power. The tactics employed are those of the schoolyard: the loudest, most abusive and most aggressive bully winds up controlling the territory (and, regrettably, the headlines).

Across multiple nations in the West today, the community's faith in the legitimacy of institutionalised political debate has collapsed. In this regard, the influence of the United States during the last decade or so has been important. The ripple effect of Trumpism has manifested in numerous ways – from the revived confidence of extremist hate groups to Scott Morrison's choice of headwear – but this American influence in fact began much earlier.

I have already noted the influence of the political behaviour modelled by Newt Gingrich, who, as speaker of the US House of Representatives from 1995 until 1999, developed a new strategy for the Republicans in opposition with his orchestration of attacks on the Clinton administration. Under Gingrich, it became standard practice to ridicule and reject any proposal that came from the Democrats, irrespective of its merits. The aim of political opposition was no longer to offer alternatives or to modify policy proposals to achieve a better result for the nation. Rather, the task was political destruction: to make it impossible for the elected government to carry out its programs. Fundamentally corrosive of democratic process, the logical end point of this strategy is one-party government.

Tony Abbott can take the credit for introducing this approach to Australia, first as leader of the opposition and then as prime minister. He systematically refused to acknowledge the legitimacy of the opposing political side and its right to propose alternatives, while pursuing crude and mendacious strategies of political attack. Abbott remains the most unrelenting and extreme exponent of this strategy, but it has been used to varying degrees by both sides of politics. This has carried substantial consequences for the rational and responsible development of national policy frameworks in Australia, with the standout example, once again, being Australia's longstanding and increasingly inexplicable failure to design a plausible policy to deal with climate change.

I wouldn't be alone in suggesting that much of the blame for this lies with the media, and the manner in which journalists have indulged, or indeed enabled, the strategies outlined above. Partly, this is due to a long-term shift towards covering politics as entertainment or sport, or as a popularity contest between individuals, rather than as a means of implementing serious policy. I published a book about the shrinkage in the ambition and focus of television news and current affairs in Australia, *Ending the Affair*,[37] back in 2005, so this shift was apparent well before that. Where once every television network had a primetime current-affairs program which took policy more or less seriously, and devoted resources to analysing it for their viewers, now it is only the ABC which remains committed to a serious focus on national public affairs (and, that, of course, has made it a rabbit in the headlights for attacks from the federal government, which determines the level of its funding).

I think it is fair to say that the trivialisation of the coverage of politics has been implicitly embraced by most politicians, notwithstanding their occasional protests to the contrary, as it makes it easier for them to direct the media's attention away from areas of policy failure or weakness. Hence the continuous stream of photo opportunities in high-vis jackets and hard hats, the spurious good news announcements, and the bursts of spin which the politicians know the media may never get around to unpacking. While the expansion of the range of media in play now may have made the management of public opinion more challenging and time-consuming, the media's diminished attention span, as well as the reduced number of journalists now covering politics, has played into the hands of those politicians who seek to deny, defer and distract.[38]

This transformed version of politics is, ironically, empowered by the fact that it lacks a genuine sense of responsibility to the public. When the media does attempt to hold government to account, their efforts are easily, even happily, stonewalled. The first response to any challenge is to pivot into campaign mode, directing the conversation towards what the opposing party 'would' do if they were in government. Next, there is the resort to policy obfuscation, such as claiming that a particular level of funding is not 'sustainable' – as if funding is determined by some kind of natural constraint, rather than being the result of political choices.

Another favourite tactic is deflection, which we see in politicians' responses to media questioning almost every day. 'I've already answered that' (when they haven't), 'that's under review/ investigation, so I can't comment', 'the other side is just playing politics', 'that's just a Canberra bubble issue', 'Australians are not interested in that – they want to know about …' and so on. Further frustrating the interviewer, a common tactic is to preface such a deflection with the phrase 'Let me be very clear about this', before launching another volley of obfuscation.

For the most part, today's politicians will never admit a mistake or acknowledge a shift in position. They will rarely apologise, and even more rarely will they display any sense of shame when challenged with revelations of misconduct or dishonesty or maladministration. Those who watch or listen to political interviews on television or radio will know that the last thing a politician wants to do is provide a definitive yes or no to a journalist's questions. (Indeed, when Anthony Albanese directly answered a question about whether or not he supported a 5 per cent increase to the minimum wage with a clear 'Absolutely', it was widely reported as a gaffe.) Instead, politicians will riff through the day's talking points to fill the time until the journalist wearies of the struggle and moves on. When challenged, they will doggedly hold to whatever policy position they have been sent out to defend, no matter how perversely blinkered the strategy might appear at the time.

Tiffen observes that the 'gladiatorial tenor' of party politics has made it impossible for any political leader to admit that he or she is uncertain about anything, or that they might need to consult or postpone a decision in order to gather more information or explore more options.[39] Judith Brett makes a similar point, in noting that our politicians' prosecution of the culture wars and the 'climate wars' have 'diminished Australian public life, too often reducing it to sterile adversarialism which prioritises anger and indignation over sympathy and compassion, and leaves little room for doubt and the compromises on which successful democracies are built'.[40]

A weakened democracy

Among the consequences of such a politics are degraded levels of transparency, probity and accountability, which were once

49

regarded as fundamental to a democratic civil society such as ours. Over 2021 and 2022, there were repeated instances of auditors' reports at both state and federal level finding that governments were misusing taxpayers' funds to advantage their own party electorally.[41] These were through grants schemes, largely, where there were inadequate checks upon the use of ministerial power to allocate funding. Public outcry has resulted, with former New South Wales Supreme Court justice Anthony Whealy, among others, reminding us that 'public money should be spent in the public interest, not for the political interests of the party in power'.[42] In 2021, Victorian Supreme Court judge David Harper described the administration of the Coalition federal government's $660-million commuter car park fund as amounting to 'corruption'.[43]

Little wonder, then, that pollsters report diminishing levels of public trust in and regard for politicians. In an Essential poll conducted at the beginning of the pandemic in 2020, at a point when there was relatively widespread acceptance of and compliance with government advice, only 19 per cent of respondents agreed that they had a strong level of trust in information from the government, indicating the 'low regard in which partisan politicians are held'.[44]

Research conducted by Professor Mark Evans, part of the Democracy 2025 initiative at the Museum of Australian Democracy at Old Parliament House, asks whether the loss of trust in government and the political class is a product of the pandemic or if it has deeper, more longstanding and therefore more worrying roots. On the one hand, Evans found, 'institutions viewed as extending the protective power of democracy in a time of fear – safeguarding our civic culture and heritage, community security, health and wellbeing – were most trusted'. For example, he reported 'high levels of trust in defence and law and order organisations such as the police (76%), army (73%) and the courts (61%)'. Interestingly, considering how little regard has been shown to these institutions by recent governments, 'the highest levels of trust are bestowed to Medicare (80%); cultural institutions such as libraries (82%) and museums (78%); and universities (70%) and experts (79%). Trust in the Australian public service also remains quite high at 55%.' [45]

There is bad news, though, for those 'institutions deemed, rightly or wrongly, to be acting on the basis of self-interest or against the collective interest': they fared worst. Significantly, in the low-scoring categories, 'politicians figure strongly. There is evidence of receding trust in political parties (20%), the national cabinet (38%) and other key institutions held responsible for bringing politics into disrepute such as television (35%), the press (30%) and especially social media (15%).'

While Evans' research tells us that there is still overwhelming support for representative democracy, it comes with a caveat about what this should mean: 'a focus on making the representative system of government more representative of the people they serve, and accountable and responsive to their constituents underpinned by integrity politics which are "cleaner", "collaborative" and "evidence-based"'. Evans concludes that the deeply rooted concerns he uncovered were about the type of society we want to live in, the values that should drive it and the form of democracy that will best protect us.[46]

Of course, Australia is not alone in this. Across the West, in recent times, we have seen the loss of trust in democratic governments opening up space for something of a boom in anti-democratic political sentiment. National leaders such as Boris Johnson and Donald Trump have presided over a degraded, self-interested political culture of 'alternative facts' and falsehoods, fuelling the public's distrust. Ironically, as these leaders have undermined the legitimacy of their national institutions in order to advance their own political interests, their behaviour has enhanced the legitimacy of those groups committed to other forms of social and political organisation.

In *How Democracies Die*, Harvard historians Steven Levitsky and Daniel Ziblatt start out by reminding their readers that when democracies are subverted, it usually happens via the ballot box – by elected autocrats rather than by more disruptive interventions such as political or military coups. Without strong allegiance to 'democratic norms', they point out, democracy can be fragile:

> Without robust norms, constitutional checks and balances do not serve as the bulwarks of democracy we imagine them to be. Institutions become political weapons, wielded forcefully by those who control them against those who do not. This is how elected autocrats subvert democracy – packing and 'weaponizing' the courts and other neutral agencies, buying off the media and the private sector (or bullying them into silence), and rewriting the rules of politics to tilt the playing field against opponents.[47]

The United States Supreme Court has offered one of the most flagrant recent examples of this, but it is not hard to find claims that Australians too are subject to such behaviour. In one example, federal Labor MP Andrew Leigh linked the Coalition government's 'attack' on charities to 'the autocrats' playbook … to suffocate civil society': both harass volunteers, shut down community organisations and restrict the operations of charities. 'The last thing a strongman needs,' he writes, 'is a group of engaged community leaders telling people the truth.'

Leigh cites a report from an international not-for-profit agency, Civicus, which tracks how individual countries treat civil society. While Australia was once in the top ranking (as an 'open' society), it has now been reclassified as 'narrowed': 'We're seeing a climate of intimidation aimed at discouraging dissent,' Civicus explained. 'Australians have always enjoyed a healthy scepticism of unchecked power, yet more recently it seems like the only people getting punished for government wrongdoing in Australia are the people who courageously reveal it.'[48] This assessment is reinforced by a thread of critical journalism which highlights what the authors characterise as a growing authoritarianism within Australia, embodied in increasingly repressive national security legislation and what Peter Greste has described as a 'war on journalism'.[49]

Levitsky and Ziblatt's discussion of the 'guardrails' of democracy – strong democratic norms – insists on the importance of the bipartisan maintenance of two key codes of conduct.[50] The first is mutual toleration of differing points of view within the political domain. That means accepting the legitimacy of those advocating a policy position even while contesting it. The routine demonisation of alternative points of view, which Australia has seen in abundance over the last two decades, breaches this code. The wilful misrepresentation of alternative points of view – again, something we have seen in abundance here – takes such a breach to another level.

The second code of conduct is what Levitsky and Ziblatt describe as 'institutional forbearance', which is largely to do with the ethical convention that a government will not use its access to institutional power in order to further its own political interests and undermine the interests of its opponents. The allocation of taxpayers' funds to grant recipients in preferred electorates, which has been labelled as 'corruption',[51] would clearly constitute an instance where that code of conduct has been breached. When the New South Wales premier Gladys Berejiklian defended her government's shameless pork-barrelling in 2021 as routine, we can only conclude that the problem has become systemic.

Levitsky and Ziblatt's historical account clearly shows that proper observance of these conventions is a key factor in enabling a democratic government to function, but such observance is in danger of being disregarded as outdated. The knock-on effects of Tony Abbott's refusal to offer such observance has demonstrated how broadly destructive that simple stance can prove.

The trashing of the convention of respecting opposing points of view may well turn out to be the most damaging instance of a broken democratic guardrail. This has taken on the most boorish and arrogant expression in recent years, with politicians not only enthusiastically indulging in such disrespect, but actually flaunting it on the floor of parliament. Judith Brett, perhaps Australia's leading academic analyst of the history of federal politics, has voiced her disgust at this attack on the dignity of the institution:

> One of the more depressing sights of the past few years was Prime Minister Morrison sitting with his back to Anthony Albanese during Question Time in June 2020. He did it again to Tanya Plibersek in October that year. We know Morrison doesn't like answering questions, especially when they come from women, but it showed an ignorant disrespect for our parliamentary traditions … Robert Menzies would never have done it.[52]

The new political culture is not serving the nation well. And the forces which have reduced politics to an insiders' game that is played at an increasing distance from the public interest have only strengthened in recent years. As a result, Australia's political culture is diminished, debased and, at its worst, plain contemptible. It is not too late for that to change, but change is definitely overdue.

The challenge to politics as usual from the successful independent candidates at the 2022 federal election suggests that the Australian people want their governments to do better. Prime Minister Albanese has promised to find a 'better way of doing politics', and his government has expressed some interest in the idea of seeking common ground rather than exploiting division. We have heard such promises before, of course. The current context, it has to be said, seems to be governed more by caution than by courage, and this should temper Australians' hopes for a wholeheartedly positive political response to the social, cultural and economic issues that have arisen over the last decade or so, and that remain unaddressed.

In addition, it seems as if the approach taken by the federal Liberal/National opposition, and to some extent the approach of the Greens, have remained more or less unaffected by what most would regard as significant shifts in the mood of the electorate. Federal opposition leader Peter Dutton has adopted an only slightly modified version of the Tony Abbott approach in his dealings with the government and the Australian people, still primarily seeking to attack Labor and recycling the standard talking points rather than engaging positively on the formation of policy. For its part, Labor, too, is shackled by its own tribal political restraints, with its dogged resistance to cooperation with the Greens on any future legislative agenda and its wary ambivalence about engaging positively with the newly elected progressive independents.

Notwithstanding such qualifications, however, and given the clear indications of the expectations of the Australian people, this must be regarded as an opportunity to repair the practice and quality of our democracy. In her late-2022 *Quarterly Essay*, journalist Katharine Murphy was notably positive in her analysis of Albanese's 'new politics' of strategic inclusivity and competent government.[53] (Even this is perhaps a sign of how low the bar is: competence has become an aspiration rather than a baseline!) Murphy is not the only member of the commentariat to express the hope that Australia might finally be making a start on renovating the culture of politics and addressing at least some aspects of the social, cultural and political malaise under which its citizens have suffered.

CHAPTER 3

Down in the hole: The consequences of neoliberalism

The Devonshire Street tunnel is the pedestrian link between Sydney's Central Station and Broadway. Pre-pandemic, it teemed with activity during peak hours. Crowds of commuters streamed through it, walking around the buskers as they headed to their destinations. Lining the sides leading to the open plaza at the Railway Square end were takeaway outlets, newsstands, a large pharmacy, cafes and coffee shops, and some small retail business shopfronts. It may have been a touch tacky, but it was vibrant. In the slightly classier cafe at the Railway Square end, on the corner beneath a stylish apartment hotel, the barista had developed the talent for delivering mini-portraits of his customers, inscribed with milk into the crema of their coffees.

In April 2022, as I walked through the tunnel at peak hour in the first week of the election campaign, it was a shock to discover how much of this had gone. The crowds of commuters had thinned and the buskers had moved on. Only two of the many food and takeaway outlets remained – a Krispy Kreme doughnuts store and a small hole-in-the-wall coffee bar. The plaza was empty and the large pharmacy had closed; a sign on its window suggested that customers might now choose to shop online. The cafe with the artistic barista was gone too, and the apartment hotel was dark and empty.

This was the time when our political and economics commentators were congratulating Australia on the 'recovery' of its economy. The standard set of macroeconomic figures suggested, they said, that the Australian economy had 'roared back to life'.[1] Try telling that to those who once earned their living in the Devonshire Street tunnel, I thought. Or to those commuters who took pleasure in the density of life they encountered on their way to work every morning. The tunnel had become an urban landscape of economic devastation, a graveyard for the hopes and efforts of those who worked there.

The fate of the Devonshire Street tunnel stands as a grim reminder of the limited adequacy of using the 'state of the economy' as a means of capturing the reality of everyday Australians' experience of the shrinking nation.

I once heard an eminent Australian economist introduce a public talk with a slightly risqué but disarmingly self-deprecating joke: 'What do economists use as a contraceptive?' he asked. 'Their personalities,' was the answer. Of course, that is not just a joke about the stereotype of the nerdy economist. It also says something about the discipline itself – commonly perceived as dry, technical, emotionless and data-driven. 'Personalities' are among the things that economics does not tell us much about.

However, it is precisely economics' technocratic bent that makes its theories and models so attractive to governments, who love the apparent certainty of the 'laws' of economics, and use them as cover for the political choices they make. But they often take economic arguments well beyond where most economists would. There are large areas of human behaviour – whole domains of contingency – which economics cannot, and does not presume to, explain. And yet, over the last few decades, one particular school of economic thought best explains what Australian governments think they have been doing as they have tried to shape the behaviour of their citizens.

In Chapter 2, I reviewed some of the technological, social and cultural changes of recent years, to which governments largely failed to respond as they defended the status quo. This chapter examines change of a very different kind, one that successive Australian governments have vigorously prosecuted through the dominant set of principles upon which they have based their management of the nation's economy.

Indebted to the theories developed by Nobel Prize–winning economist Milton Friedman, pump-primed by the notorious 'trickle-down' promise of President Ronald Reagan's 'Reaganomics', and initially championed by governments in the 1980s and 1990s as 'economic rationalism',[2] this approach has more recently acquired the label of 'neoliberalism'.[3] Its core components are a commitment to small government, lower taxes, cuts in government spending aimed at a balanced budget, and a reliance upon the market, rather than on government, to deliver services and opportunities. Neoliberalism is interested in supporting the individual rather than the community, the private sector rather than the public sector, and the economy rather than the nation.

We have had at least thirty years of the major parties' political alignment with the key tenets of neoliberalism. The implementation of these tenets – although selective and in many cases motivated more by political self-interest than by purely economic objectives – has had a substantial economic impact. It is important to recognise, however, that the impact of neoliberalism is more than economic. Neoliberalism has changed Australian society and culture, and its consequences are becoming ever more concerning. So although the conventional narratives about neoliberalism in Australia are about macroeconomic structures, there is also another story to tell. That story only reveals itself when we look at how the legacies of neoliberalism have changed the daily lives of millions of Australian citizens.

It is important to appreciate how an exclusively economic accounting for the consequences of neoliberalism has minimised our recognition of its impact on our lived experience. It has distracted us from understanding how the project of neoliberalism has altered our social conditions and repositioned the citizen within the national culture – what social scientist Michael Pusey has described as 'the dark side' of economic reform.[4] We now hear much about rising inequality in Australia, and see its trajectory represented in graphs and percentages in media commentary depicting stagnating wages, wealth and income transfer and so on. However, seeing inequality only as an economic issue draws its teeth. The abstraction of the economic accounts allows us to overlook the human consequences. These are not only about surviving on low wages, or covering the cost of childcare, or securing an education, or dealing with the material consequences of social, geographic, physical or financial disadvantage. They are also about how Australians must now think about their lives and their futures.

For instance, if our young people now find that Australia is offering them less than it offered their parents; if they can no longer realistically expect to own their own home; if they are saddled with substantial long-term debt as soon as they leave university; if they find that even those government safety nets they can access are punitively administered and socially stigmatising;

and if they see their employment options as offering no way out of this situation, then that constitutes not just an economic shift but a significant social and cultural change that will resonate within that generation's lives for the foreseeable future. Add to this the years of putting their lives on hold as they wait out the pandemic before resuming their education or getting on with their careers and reconnecting with their communities, and we can see just how life-changing all of this has been.

The effects of the long experiment with small government, low taxes, spending cuts, market fundamentalism and the political strategy of holding the individual entirely responsible for the conditions in which they live are part of the story of the shrinking nation. In addition to the social and political consequences of rising inequality, Richard Denniss claims, 'the neoliberal agenda of "free markets", "free trade" and "trickle-down tax cuts" has wounded our national identity, bled our national confidence, caused paralysis in our parliaments, and is eating away at the identity of those on the right of Australian politics'.[5] It is not only the identity of those on the right of Australian politics that is being undermined here; neoliberalism is eating away at the sense of security and national belonging once regarded as fundamental to national citizenship.

The end of the great neoliberal experiment

In his *Quarterly Essay* 'Exit Strategy: Politics after the pandemic', George Megalogenis records what he describes as the United States reaching 'a historic moment of self-awareness, brought on by the pandemic: the model of capitalism authored by Ronald Reagan is over':

'Trickle-down economics has never worked,' Joe Biden declared in his first address as president to a joint session of Congress in April, 'and it is time to grow the economy from the bottom and the middle out.' The statement would have been unremarkable if made by an economist. The idea that Reaganomics relied on a confidence trick has been understood in academic circles for some years. But Biden is the first US leader prepared to call neoliberalism's bluff by deliberately increasing the size of government, and paying for it, in part, with higher taxes on companies and individuals.[6]

Biden is not the only former proponent to now take such a view. Former prime minister Kevin Rudd is even more definitive in his assessment: 'The great neoliberal experiment of the last thirty years has failed. Neoliberalism and the free market fundamentalism it produced have been revealed as little more than personal greed dressed up as economic philosophy.'[7] Denniss expresses a similar view: neoliberalism is 'the ideal cloak behind which to conceal enormous shifts in Australia's wealth and culture', as it provides 'powerful people with the perfect language in which to dress up their self-interest as the national interest'.[8]

I want to start by pulling this cloak aside, in order to explain how each of the core tenets of the neoliberal agenda has been discredited over the last decade or so. This first section of the chapter will draw particularly upon Richard Denniss's commentary, as he has been a prolific public critic of the politics of neoliberalism. His professional indignation at the enormity of the 'confidence trick' is palpable. 'Australians have been told,' he says, 'we can't afford high-quality public services, that public ownership of assets is inefficient, and that the pursuit of free markets through deregulation would create wealth and prosperity for all. But none of this is true.'[9]

Also untrue is the proposition that providing major tax cuts for the rich increases the general level of wealth and prosperity, via the 'trickle-down' effect, which says that the benefits will work their way through the economy. There is no evidence, in fact, that tax cuts for the rich generate any significant benefit at all to the economy's growth or to employment levels. There is evidence, however, that they actually play a significant role in increasing inequality.[10]

Furthermore, there is strong evidence that taking the opposite approach – increasing taxes on the wealthy – works to redistribute income and can have a positively transformative effect on society. Of course, designing the tax system so that it might redistribute income is not popular with those who most benefit from the current arrangements. Limiting debates over such a reform to economic concerns is among the means they employ to relegate the social, cultural and democratic concerns around taxation to the status of second-order issues.

The political prioritising of the economy and the interests of business has in part been due to a substantial rethinking of the social function of business, which took off during the 1970s. Milton Friedman controversially proposed that the primary purpose of business, in addition to providing goods and opportunities to the society, was to build value for their shareholders.[11] This influential idea has resulted in such a thoroughgoing transformation of the political conception of the social function of business – in effect, that the maximisation of profit constitutes a public good in itself – that it is hard to remember when it was any other way.

Paul Collier and John Kay, in their optimistically titled book *Greed Is Dead: Politics after individualism*, remind us that there was a time when the only basis on which corporate organisations could claim legitimacy in a democratic society was that they delivered goods and services which people wanted, and provided satisfying and rewarding employment to many. Once we move beyond that justification, they insist, 'there is no adequate answer to the question of legitimacy provoked by [Milton] Friedman's assertion that the social responsibility of business is to extract as much profit as possible from the community'. And if that is indeed the proposition, Collier and Kay ask, then 'why should we allow them to do that'?[12]

Australian political commentator Bernard Keane might sympathise with that question. He delivers a withering takedown of the part played by the political deference to the self-interest of business in generating the mess we're in, as a result of decades of neoliberal policy settings:

> Australia's business leaders are always wanting to know what you've done for them lately. There are always more taxes that must be cut, more workers whose wages must be reduced, and more regulations that must be stripped back – and always urgently, lest economic doom overtake us. Australia's corporate sector insists unions are 'out of control', Australia is a 'high cost economy', real wages 'have to fall', company taxes must be slashed, while ever more deregulation is needed to save capitalism from being strangled by red tape. There's always another country that has lower taxes, lower wages, less regulation than us. 'Time to give business a break', the country's chief business lobby group demanded before the 2016 election, as if they had been the victims of 30 years of reform, not the beneficiaries.[13]

It is easy to see these as standard components of the push and pull between labour and capital in this country. The surprising thing, perhaps, is that such sophistry has been so successful for so long. Among the means through which business sought to legitimise its claim to represent the interests of the nation was a philosophical shift which took us away from thinking of the individual as responsible to the community, and towards a much more radical individualism, one that validated behaviour driven, as Rudd suggests, simply by self-interest. Achieving this shift has been a conservative project for a very long time. Way back in 1963, in the United States, JK Galbraith was mocking conservatives for being engaged in one of the 'oldest, best financed, most applauded, and, on the whole, least successful exercises in moral philosophy. That is, the search for a truly superior moral justification for selfishness.'[14] Collier and Kay's *Greed Is Dead* suggests that while this mission may have attracted many adherents over time, that support is now running out. Their observations indicate that the extreme individualism embraced by many prominent and successful people in recent decades is no longer tenable. Even if, as they argue, such reductive accounts of the point of the corporation bore little relation to the reality of how many successful modern businesses actually functioned,[15] the theory was so politically and economically influential that we have now reached the point where 'it has all gone much too far'.[16]

Similarly, it would seem, with the much touted reliance on the market as the most efficient means of distributing opportunities, services and wealth. Especially as a result of lessons learned during the pandemic, there is diminishing support for this component of the neoliberal agenda. Small government, to the extent that it actually occurred in Australia, was largely about cutting government spending, outsourcing services to the market and offloading assets through programs of privatisation. The consequences for social services and health provision, as well as for the maintenance of emergency relief services, for instance, have proven disastrous when placed under pressure by the Black Summer bushfires, repeated flood events over 2021 and 2022, and three years of the pandemic.

In addition, the much publicised failure of so many privatisation projects to deliver services that were even close to adequate in recent years – most scandalously in aged-care homes, disability services and childcare businesses – has demonstrated how unsatisfactory the market can be when providing essential services for profit. Former Liberal Party leader John Hewson has lamented that much of the merit behind the idea of privatisation 'has been lost through greed'[17] – either by government seeking maximum revenue without sufficient guarantees on the quality of service to be provided, or by the private providers exploiting the weakness of government oversight to compromise the quality of their services in pursuit of greater profits.

And even if the markets did work more rationally, the French economist Thomas Piketty argues, that would not be enough. '[R]eal democracy and social justice require specific institutions of their own,' he says, 'not just those of the market, and not just parliaments and other formal democratic institutions.' This is because (and this certainly should give us pause) 'capitalism automatically generates arbitrary and unsustainable inequalities that radically undermine the meritocratic values on which democratic societies are based'.[18]

Political scientist Keith Dowding's critique of neoliberalism focuses upon how it has driven changes in more traditional conceptions of the role of government. According to Dowding, the role of government has shrunk dramatically over the last forty years because it has shifted responsibility for the conditions in which we live – housing, health, employment, social welfare and so on – onto the individual. This leads, he says, 'to the idea that the responsibility for social problems lies with people and not the government'. Governments around the world, including Australia, have progressively relinquished their interest in securing the welfare of the nation's citizens.

Central to this trend has been the rising influence of political theories of individualism.[19] As Judith Brett has written, neoliberalism assumed a 'particular form of human subjectivity, the rational, opportunity-maximising, self-interested individual … who is primarily motivated by competition in their working and public life'.[20] Under the influence of what Dowding calls the 'cult of personal responsibility', governments have shifted the burden of responsibility first from the government to the market, and then to the choices made by the individual consumer. Their belief in marketisation has provided the rationale that allows governments to 'get out of the way' – leaving the market to 'decide' and consumers to 'freely' choose, while winding back regulations that might protect consumers or level the playing field for producers. Such a rationale makes a number of key assumptions: that everyone in the market has perfect information, that there are no monopolies or companies that dominate the markets, and that there is no cost to entering or exiting the market. None of these assumptions, says Dowding, fit the reality.[21]

The payoff for governments is clear: they have found a means of blaming citizens for failures that are actually the structural consequences of governmental policies. It's a neat trick: when things go wrong, people only have themselves to blame.

Dowding examines some of the negative consequences of the enthusiasm for small government, arguing that 'the welfare of people in liberal democracies has greatly diminished as governments have got out of the business of looking after their citizens'. Over the last forty years, he claims, governments 'have not only failed to keep up with what is happening in markets that serve their citizens badly and failed to regulate in ways which are socially optimal, but they have actively pursued policies that have created more social problems'.[22] He demonstrates this, powerfully, through a series of focused Australian case studies relating to gun crime, obesity, homelessness and problem gambling.

A more left-field attack on neoliberal economics comes from modern monetary theory (MMT), which criticises the myths used to demonise government deficits and increased public spending, while unpicking the false analogy so often disingenuously drawn between the economy of the domestic household and that of the nation (for a start, households can't print their own money). In her (unlikely) global bestseller *The Deficit Myth: Modern monetary theory and how to build a better economy*, Stephanie Kelton claims that 'in almost all instances, federal deficits are good for the economy. They are necessary. And the way we have thought about them and treated them is often incomplete or inaccurate.' Rather than chasing the 'misguided goal of a balanced budget', she continues, 'we should be pursuing the promise of what MMT calls our public money, or sovereign currency, to balance the economy so that prosperity is broadly shared and not concentrated in fewer and fewer hands'.[23]

While the melody of neoliberalism lingers, there are not nearly so many singing along anymore. It has taken a long time for the outcomes of the great neoliberal experiment to clearly manifest themselves, and even longer for them to be acknowledged by its authors, but they are now difficult to ignore or misrepresent. What remains is the need for some kind of reckoning, a direct confrontation of the harm that has been done.

From trickle-down to siphoning up

In his book *Populism Now! The case for progressive populism* David McKnight provides a personal account that goes to the core of this issue: just how fundamentally the lived experience of ordinary Australians has changed over these years:

I grew up in a single-income, blue-collar family with my mother suffering from a severe mental illness. Yet we survived and thrived thanks in part to a strong public sector, especially in health and education. This public sector was grounded in the major parties' consensus that it was both morally obligatory and economically sound that important public services should be equally available to all and provided collectively. Now this consensus is being broken apart and discarded … [I]n terms of simple practical things such as expecting a secure well-paid job, social services and a home to live in, we are going backward.[24]

Populism Now! examines the social and cultural consequences of neoliberalism. It focuses on the rise of the 'super-rich' and increasing patterns of income inequality, the reconfiguration of work (with particular reference to casualisation and the exploitation of temporary workers' visas in Australia), the consequences of government policies on housing investment, and the privileging of the interests of sectors such as finance and resources over the common good. McKnight argues that the orthodoxies of deregulation and privatisation have radically transformed Australia, widening the gulf between the 'billionaires and the poor' as the 'old egalitarian Australia crumbles'.[25] The great beneficiaries of this era have been the wealthy elite and those in the upper income brackets, while the losers have been ordinary Australians on low or middle incomes. In the workplace, McKnight notes, 'jobs are less secure; there is a far greater proportion of casual and part-time work, and under-employment is surging'.[26]

McKnight's assessment is at times personal and often polemical. But what he tells us is strongly supported by empirical research coming out of sociology and social history. Warr, Jacobs and Paternoster, for instance, offer this thumbnail sketch of the effects of the neoliberal agenda on the lives of Australians – effects they argue were already becoming evident in the 'closing decades of the twentieth century':

> Amid processes of deindustrialization as manufacturing moved offshore, the casualization of labour markets, the winding back of the welfare state, and the disintegration of working-class socio-political formations, such as the trade unions, the everyday lives of many working class people, and their communities, were transforming. As economic security declined, neoliberal tenets emphasized personal and local responsibility … implying that situations of poverty and relative disadvantage can be attributed to individual failings such as poor choices, imprudent behaviour and ignorance …[27]

Gerrard and Threadgold's more contemporary sociological discussion of the shifting formations of class in Australia paints a similar picture:

> Like most advanced capitalist countries, Australia has now reached a point where current generations inherit a lower standard of living than their parents, in relative terms. According to measures of inequality, the rich/poor gap is widening, returning to the heights of the 1920s … Education is getting more expensive, while social welfare is increasingly difficult to access, and is punitively administered. While political slogans about 'a fair go' and egalitarianism still abound, the reality for anyone who is not from a privileged, well connected background is exclusion from the housing market, and the prospect of insecure work in a labour market that demands 'flexibility', 'employability', 'creativity' and 'innovation'. These neoliberal buzzwords are really ciphers for upper-middle-class qualifications and dispositions. For the majority of working people in Australia, experience of economic

precarity and livelihood anxiety had become the norm even before the COVID-19 pandemic.[28]

This accurately reflects the clear consensus among researchers across many disciplines, and also among many public commentators on Australian politics, that the rise in social inequality is foremost among the worrying social changes that have occurred over this period. There are many aspects to this – and the treatment of the unemployed, the underemployment of (in particular) women, and the legacies of decades of enforced 'wage restraint' are all long-term factors.

There is also, however, a relatively recent element. There is a growing underclass of poorly paid, casual or precariously employed workers. A key element in this has been the exploitation of those in Australia on temporary work visas, who tend to provide contracted labour and are thus outside the award systems. The growth of this sector has played a part in driving down wages elsewhere in the economy. More broadly, though, the growth of casualisation and the development of the gig economy have exposed the loopholes in current industrial relations regulations, creating new industrial behaviours that sidestep employers' obligations to pay award wages, as well as standard employee entitlements such as recreational and sick leave.

As Gerrard and Threadgold note above, the promotion of the gig economy through buzzwords such as 'flexibility', 'innovation' and 'creativity' has disguised the real dangers to the individual that come from living with precarity. It is significant that a new crime of 'wage theft' has been proposed as a desirable addition to the statute books, to counteract the widespread and systemic underpayment of casual workers in industries such as hospitality and agriculture – although it has also been revealed to be common in higher education, where many millions of dollars are currently being paid as restitution to underpaid casual teaching and administration staff.

Even when award wages are paid, wage levels have remained static, failing to keep pace with increases in the cost of living. We are finding that lower-paid people – the 'working poor' – find it hard to avoid sinking ever deeper into poverty traps. At the same time, executive salaries and bonuses have, notoriously, boomed.

Australians do not have to tolerate this situation. The government support paid in the first phase of the pandemic proved to be an accidental test case, which revealed very clearly how policymakers might go about improving conditions for those at the lower end of the wage scale. A report produced by UNSW Sydney and ACOSS in 2022, titled *Covid, Inequality and Poverty in 2020 & 2021*, found that the crisis support payments paid during the initial coronavirus wave in 2020 – in particular, the doubling of payments to the unemployed – had a dramatic effect, halving poverty and significantly reducing income equality. When these payments were discontinued without the provision of any adequate substitute, the number of people in poverty shot up again by 20 per cent, and income inequality increased – partly due to a bias towards jobs growth in high-paid jobs and a rapid rise in investment incomes.[29]

As noted earlier, the gap between rich and poor has increased substantially over the last decade or so.[30] This is increasingly impacting on the life prospects of younger Australians. While this is widely acknowledged, there is little on the policy horizon that seems likely to address the problem. 'Our young people,' says Bernard Keane, 'are set to be our most screwed-over, betrayed and exploited generation since the 1930s. They're the targets of a generational war waged by the rest of us.'[31] He points to the knock-on effects of a 'badly skewed property market' as one of the primary battlegrounds of this war:

> It is economically and socially dislocative: to access jobs and other
> economic opportunities, young people and low-income earners
> must work in areas where they can't afford to buy, meaning they
> rent forever or spend much of their time trapped in gridlocked
> infrastructure trying to get to their jobs. And services that need
> low- and middle-income earning employees – health care,
> childcare, aged care, education – struggle to attract staff because
> the people they would normally recruit live dozens of kilometres
> and 90 minutes away by car.[32]

Locked out of the opportunity to acquire what was previously the
most widely distributed form of personal wealth, today's young
people face a far worse situation than their parents. Nobody really
knows what the social consequences of this will be in the medium
to long term, but they can't be good. Any hope of upward social
mobility – which has long been a fundamental aspiration for
many in our communities, and part of the dynamics of progressive
social change – is rendered illusory.

There are many other constituencies upon whom we could
focus as having failed to benefit from growth in the economy. The
cost of childcare, the continuing discrimination against women in
certain industries, and the persistence of sexual harassment in the
workplace and the explosion of domestic violence at home have
compromised progress towards gender equality. The introduction
of the National Disability Insurance Scheme (NDIS) aimed to
protect those disadvantaged by disability, but there have been a
litany of complaints about how this is currently managed, about
arbitrary (and often automated) decisions on changes to support
for individual recipients, and about the massive underspend in the
allocations made for the program. What can only be described as
a stubborn class divide which splits the city of Sydney into east
and west was dramatically, and lethally, revealed by the variation

in the state government strategies employed during the spread of the Delta strain of Covid-19 in 2020–21. Structural inequalities which affected the capacity of citizens in western Sydney to evade the virus – they were less able to work from home, to avoid public transport or to home-school their children, as many of them, ironically, were deemed 'essential workers' – meant that their region suffered disproportionately from extended lockdowns and excess hospitalisations and deaths.

Within rural communities, perhaps the longest-running and seemingly most intractable social change has been the increasing gap between the level of services provided to rural and metropolitan areas by both federal and state administrations. The commercialisation of the services sector, in particular, has had a massively disproportionate effect on rural and regional communities. Net migration from these communities to the city may have been temporarily stalled by the influx of tree-changers and sea-changers during the pandemic, but it is likely that many of these former city dwellers will be shocked when they try to connect to high-speed internet, find reliable mobile coverage, book an appointment with a GP, access social welfare services, schedule elective surgery, enjoy an uninterrupted supply of electricity, buy a local newspaper, acquire affordable rental accommodation or find a local branch of their bank.

And for those who have always lived and worked in rural areas, the challenge has become to find ways of surviving economically as their businesses have been severely affected by the restrictions on domestic movement and immigration, as well as by the reduced supply of backpacking tourists and international students, who once provided valuable seasonal labour.

The 2022 floods in the Northern Rivers region of New South Wales provided yet another example of just how little concern state and federal governments have for the wellbeing of their country residents. The lack of urgency apparent in the delayed provision of relief services to these communities was disgraceful and, for those affected, devastating. Talk radio host Ben Fordham spoke for many when he expressed his alarm at this situation during an interview with Prime Minister Morrison in March 2022, protesting that 'we are not a third-world country'. As he implied, Australians are entitled to expect better than this.

It is now frequently suggested that Australia has become a more divided community than previously was the case. If this is true, the divisions are not just across class lines but increasingly across generations, between genders, between the country and the city, and around the social and cultural values attributed to various forms of ethnicity. The political strategies discussed in Chapter 2, whereby politicians seek to divide communities in order to target their own constituencies, have been very effective; culture wars are easily ignited and require little in the way of evidence. The result is that many Australians who find themselves on the wrong side of these divides have been made to feel that the government is not in their corner, and that they must deal with whatever challenges arise in their lives on their own. This is an alienating and corrosive experience.

In *Dead Right*, Richard Denniss talks at some length about how we might understand the non-material consequences of neoliberalism. The fact that governments have sought to mobilise fear as a means of gaining support for their positions, he argues, means that Australians are now existentially afraid – of losing their jobs or their welfare benefits, and of what might be their likely futures. Their governments see no value in reassuring them; indeed, Denniss claims, fear 'gives people an incentive' – the rationale behind decades of deliberately inadequate unemployment benefits. Consequently, Denniss goes on, 'Australia isn't a relaxed country anymore; it is a country full of busy, stressed and insecure people, who worry when business high-flyers tell them that if they don't work harder, they will be replaced by someone who will work for less'.

The community spirit so often seen as central to Australian culture and society has started to look like an anachronism. The neoliberal value of looking after yourself first is fundamentally incompatible with the value of 'sticking by your mates when times are tough'. At the level of policy development, Denniss says, the embedding of this form of self-interested individualism has been transformative. To our cost, he concludes, 'trickle-down economics has been incredibly effective in shifting our national debate away from what government policies are right, fair or necessary and towards a permanent conversation about which policies are affordable, efficient and provide people with the right incentives'.[33]

There are some – maybe many – who would contest or qualify Denniss's account of neoliberalism.[34] Some of this debate relies on an expertise in economics that I cannot claim to possess. However, looking at this as a cultural historian, I find it hard to disagree with the view that the two foundational tribal myths of neoliberalism (small government and market fundamentalism) run against the grain of some of the core mythologies which inform Australians' sense of their national identities and public values. An emphasis on competition and individualism does not sit comfortably alongside the values of cooperation, community, egalitarian solidarity and personal self-sacrifice that are routinely mobilised in our narratives of what makes Australian history and society distinctive. Consequently, their continued influence is likely to result in a very different culture to the one we might have thought we inhabited some years ago. Markets are not at all egalitarian structures, and small government does not build nations. It is time we thought more critically about how these ideas have affected the purchase of cultural values once held to be fundamental to the formation of this national community, and why that might matter.

The shrinking state and the provisional citizen

It may be a sign of the times that a book such as Michael Lewis's *The Fifth Risk: Undoing democracy* needed to be written.[35] While on the one hand presenting as an inside account of the shredding of federal public administration in the United States during Donald Trump's presidency, along the way the book carefully assembles a mountain of evidence about how fundamentally necessary the work of government is for sustaining people's wellbeing and for the effective functioning of society.

For an American readership, that mountain of evidence is clearly needed. Americans' faith in their government's capacity to improve people's lives, which has steadily declined since Ronald Reagan was president, must be revived if they are to find a path out of their current dysfunction. The state of democracy in the United States provides us with a worrying glimpse into a possible future for us too, as 'the incessant propaganda war against the efficiency and effectiveness of government services, combined with the obsession with shrinking the size and role of governments, is now helping to drive a loss of faith in democracy itself', as Richard Denniss notes.[36] For some years now, opportunistic conservatives in Australia have been actively importing some of that anti-government rhetoric, enlisting its slogans and 'alternative facts' to an effort to make the beneficiaries of small government look like personifications of the national interest. However, the recent combination of fires, floods and pandemic has made such talk, to most commentators, seem ridiculous. No one requiring urgent access to a hospital bed or emergency disaster relief is likely to agree that it would be a good idea for government to 'get out of the way'.

However, there has been more than enough of that talk, and enough of its influence on policy, to have had a seriously deleterious effect. 'A major casualty of neoliberalism,' writes Judith Brett, 'has been the capacity of the federal government to deliver services, as it privatised and outsourced many of its responsibilities. Steering not rowing was the mantra. Government would pay the bills for the private sector to do the work.'[37]

Earlier on, in his 2005 account of the state of the nation, Anthony Moran related this tendency to the nation-state's response to globalisation, which he said resulted in the political choices made around decisions on taxation (such as reducing corporate and higher personal income taxation), reductions in spending (especially on social welfare), and the decision to privatise government services and utilities. As a result of these choices, he writes, 'hospitals, schools, rail lines, banks, post offices, and other services disappeared from many rural areas and suburbs of the cities in Australia in the 1980s and 1990s'.[38] This process has only gathered pace over the last decade; see, for instance, journalist Andrew Taylor's commentary on the 'pure greed' driving rural bank closures in recent years.[39]

Nonetheless, as neoliberalism gained traction among policymakers, it was not the forces of globalisation that were most in play when the potential social implications of the state removing itself were largely set aside in favour of profits and the facilitation of private commercial interests.[40] As we have seen, this was to do with the philosophical shift towards individualism and the influence of market fundamentalism. Under their influence, and with government now being cast 'as the problem rather than the solution', as John Quiggin observes, 'it was easier for the Commonwealth to shift tasks seen as peripheral back to the states, or hand them over to the private sector through privatisation and contracting'. This left the federal government free to focus on what the political class saw as 'big picture' issues, 'such as foreign policy and macroeconomic management'.[41]

The result is evident in the topic Quiggin addresses in 'Dismembering Government', his 2021 essay in *The Monthly*: 'why the Commonwealth government can't do anything anymore'. The coronavirus crisis has revealed huge gaps in state capacity,[42] leading to the widespread conclusion that 'the Commonwealth doesn't do things'. While that would certainly be accepted as a valid observation today, this is a relatively recent development. As Michael Pusey put it right at the beginning of all this, our 'nation-building state' has 'changed its mind'.[43]

In order to illustrate just how much has changed as a result of this shift in the interests of the state, Quiggin asks readers to suppose that, during our experience of the pandemic, we were led by a Commonwealth government with capabilities similar to the one we had fifty years ago. Back then, the Commonwealth still operated its own quarantine facilities and had its own Department of Works, which was 'capable of building new facilities or expanding old ones'. It had extensive experience in managing large-scale and complicated initiatives, such as the repatriation of hundreds of thousands of troops from World War II and the provision of housing to support 'an immigration program on an unparalleled scale'. The Commonwealth also ran its own network of repatriation hospitals and owned the Commonwealth Serum Laboratories (CSL), while vaccinations (such as for smallpox) were a part of everyday life and relatively uncontroversial. Above all, Quiggin argues:

> the Commonwealth government had confidence in its own capacity, employing the best and brightest graduates

of the universities that had expanded massively thanks to Commonwealth funding beginning in the 1960s. The Commonwealth government saw itself as both more competent and less subject to interest group pressure than the states. Under both conservative and Labor governments, the Commonwealth had steadily expanded the scope and scale of its operations, reducing the roles of both state governments and the business sector. [44]

If that kind of government had been in power over the past three years, we might have expected a 'national response' to the coronavirus, including requirements for Qantas (formerly government-owned) to repatriate Australians from overseas, a rapid expansion of dedicated quarantine facilities, and a consistent national policy on lockdowns and movement restrictions. Of course, says Quiggin, 'we have seen nothing like this … the Commonwealth has sought to avoid responsibility, and transfer it either to the states or to private parties ranging from management consultants to hotel operators'.[45]

Interestingly, as the Commonwealth has got out of the way, state governments have taken on a more active role, and can be seen to be 'running a separate and far more ambitious agenda than the Commonwealth'.[46] On, for instance, issues such as climate change, they appear to have taken their responsibility to the electorate more seriously than their federal counterparts. Quiggin's example of this rests on the comparison between the private market in aged-care services run by the Commonwealth, and the public system in Victoria run by the state government:

During the difficult second-wave Melbourne COVID-19 outbreak, the inadequacy of the private aged-care system became horribly evident, as it accounted for the vast majority (82 per cent) of total COVID-related deaths. Understaffing and reliance on casuals working across several facilities were crucial factors. State-run facilities had only a handful of cases. While this outcome was partly due to geographical factors (the state-run facilities are more heavily concentrated in regional areas less exposed to the pandemic), the recent royal commission into aged care exposed systematic deficiencies, particularly in the for-profit sector.[47]

The divisiveness of contemporary politics, and the rising sense that the federal government no longer cares about citizens' wellbeing, may well be contributing to the formation of a much more provisional understanding of what our entitlements or expectations might be as an Australian citizen. If we needed a demonstration of just how provisional that status has become, we need only look to the federal government's restrictions on travel for Australian citizens during the first two years of Covid.

Australia is the only nation-state which not only refused to allow tens of thousands of its citizens to return home as they sought refuge from the pandemic or attempted to reunite with their families, but also banned citizens, temporary visa holders, permanent residents and dual citizens from leaving the country. To do otherwise, we were told, would place too much pressure on Australia's (almost non-existent) quarantine capacity. This edict was reinforced by the introduction of massive fines for anyone who might find a means of evading these restrictions (and get caught). As a challenge to the sense of national belonging felt by Australians, as well as to their human rights as citizens of a sovereign nation, it is hard to imagine anything the Commonwealth could do which would more fundamentally undermine confidence in government.

Of course, for our most vulnerable citizens – those in aged care or requiring disability services, for instance – the impression that they were less deserving than others has been reinforced by the many failures in government services and attention. As Denniss points out, there is an implicit hierarchy in how our citizens are viewed within the prism of government support structures:

> Neoliberalism has trained Australians to focus on how deserving individuals are, rather than on how caring we think our society should be. We take it for granted that pensioners get more income support than the disabled, who in turn get more than the sick, who in turn get more than the unemployed.[48]

These days for Australians, national citizenship, like nostalgia, is not what it used to be.

A personal postscript

Much of the research and writing in which I was involved during the 1980s and 1990s was investigating the idea of the nation, and versions of Australian nationalism. My Baby Boomer generation had grown up within a nation that faced towards the United Kingdom and was led by a patrician Anglophile in Sir Robert Menzies, but it was also oriented towards a pragmatic project of nation-building, centring on the development of infrastructure and the establishment of the institutions of a civil society. The election of the Whitlam government in 1972 released a burst of cultural nationalism that had been slowly building over these years, with aspirations towards the development of a more independent and distinctive culture and society. This tendency sputtered a little during the subsequent Fraser government, but came back to life during the Hawke/Keating administrations. The cultural nationalist surge across the creative and entertainment industries culminated with the centralising of cultural policy within the nation's political agenda and the release of Keating's *Creative Nation* in 1994.[49]

However, the economic rationalism that also emerged during this period ran against the grain of that cultural nationalist surge – not just in economic terms, but also in the manner in which it set out to reposition the social and the cultural within the meaning of the nation. The shift in the meanings of the nation that economic rationalism generated was incremental, and so it took a while for its implications to become evident. But the contradiction it embodied for Australian culture over the 1980s attracted my interest. In looking at how the discourses and meanings of nationalism were appropriated by particular sets of interests for my book *Making It National: Nationalism and Australian popular culture* (1994), I came across many warning signs which pointed towards the kind of social and cultural consequences outlined in the preceding parts of this chapter.[50]

They were noticeable, I thought, in the high profile accorded to a group of businessmen who became identified with the unlikely 'homology between an aggressive entrepreneurial business ethic and conventional definitions of the Australian character'.[51] The figures of Alan Bond, John Elliott and Mike Gore, in particular, achieved much of their popular prominence by riding that wave of cultural nationalism to become national figures. Bond's celebrity was, of course, tied to his national hero status as the winner of the America's Cup yacht race, but the fact that such uncompromisingly rapacious entrepreneurs were able to achieve this kind of status was nonetheless surprising, in light of what my research had revealed about Australians' historical suspicion of capitalism and lack of respect for business:

When one goes back through the *Bulletin*'s early decades the hated figure of the 'fat capitalist' crops up at every point, from the cartoons to the leaders. During the Depression, the figure of the 'foreign banker' is similarly pilloried in the popular press – usually in terms we would now recognize as anti-Semitic – reinforcing popular explanations for the severity of the Depression which blamed the influence of overseas bankers on the domestic economy. There seemed to be little question then that the interests of international business and those of Australia were fundamentally opposed.[52]

Given the traditional Australian view that 'anyone whose life was dominated by the making of money had to be doing so at someone else's expense and therefore could not be trusted',[53] there was some point in examining how this judgement was modified during the 1980s as discourses of 'the nation' gradually gave way to 'the economy'.[54]

The men I called the 'larrikin capitalists' each combined an aggressive entrepreneurialism (they tended to be takeover merchants) with aspects of what looked like an authentically Australian masculine identity. Bond was the classic immigrant made good, Elliott was the larrikin boozer (notwithstanding his privileged background), while Gore was the beer-gutted wide boy credited with leading the Gold Coast's 'white-shoe brigade' of real estate developers. Each of these 'star businessmen' was sold to the Australian public as an anti-authoritarian upstart, 'working against tradition in one location or another' and taking on the world. They were widely endorsed as the forerunners of a 'new, aggressively Australian, version of capitalism'.[55] Through their public representations, the signifiers of enterprise, the acquisition of personal wealth (well, greed, really) and an Australian national identity merged into one. Eventually, of course, they all crashed and burned as that moment passed, but their period in the spotlight softened us up, in a sense, for what was coming next.

And what was coming next takes us back to the narrative outlined earlier in this chapter: the neoliberal redefinition of the social function of business. This wasn't accomplished only by way of the theoretical shift around individualism we discussed earlier: it also involved the introduction of a restricted and highly ideological lexicon for talking about the relations between business, society and the nation. The shifts in the framing of the leading edge of international capitalism during the 'greed is good' decade represented business in new ways that promoted the competitive, the pragmatic and the unfettered. The vanguard of this new version of business were the 'hard men': 'the ones who draw their knowledge from "the real world" in order to make the "tough decisions" that would affect "every Australian's life"'.[56] Counterintuitively, 'the market' became the place where we found the 'real world':

> [I]ndeed, the 'market' was talked about as if it were not the theoretical abstraction it is – as if one could actually *go* there any time. The alternatives to market forces –'social planning' or, worse, 'social engineering' – were talked about as if they were a little like 'family planning' or 'genetic engineering': as, respectively, dated and moralistic or pejoratively academic interventions into the natural order of things.[57]

At the same time, according to sociologist Michael Emmison, writing in 1983, the needs of the economy were being constructed as 'eternal', as above the concerns of politics. In this way, Emmison argued, unpopular political decisions could be taken and policies justified while avoiding the charge that they were serving class or sectional interests. In what turned out to be a prescient analysis of the strategies that would be employed by neoliberalism over the succeeding decades, Emmison noted that when specific social or political choices are presented as the irresistible effects of 'the inexorable workings of the market', the nation's economy becomes 'more important than its citizens'.[58]

As I summed all this up in the early 1990s, it seemed clear that no good was going to come from this economistic reconstruction of the nation, and the manner in which the needs of the economy and the interests of business would likely drive Australian politics and society over the following decades. The anti-statism of the dominant trends in international business, the dogged commitment to the overarching principle of the free play of the market, and what seemed to me then as the inevitable conflict between the exclusively commercial interests of a globalised market and the broader political, social and cultural interests of the sovereign nation-state all loomed as problems for the future.

Actually, not just for the future. When I re-read *Making It National* now, almost thirty years on, it is disconcerting to be reminded that the consequences this chapter has discussed were apparent even then. The closing paragraph of my chapter on the larrikin capitalists refers to what had already begun to change as a result of the reshaping of the relation between business, the culture and the state over this period: there had been 'a radical redistribution of wealth in Australia over the last ten years', I wrote, 'and ... business has made real gains in extricating itself from state control'.[59]

Today, it is clear that this power relation has been reversed. Now the task confronting the nation-state is to extract itself from the influence of corporate and financial power, the resources industries and the peak bodies representing the interests of big business and the banks, in order to fulfil the much greater commitment it has to serve the needs and welfare of its citizens. All of them. Such as those who once worked in the Devonshire Street tunnel.

CHAPTER 4

Media and information 2.0: What we know now, and how we know it

'[A]t the very moment when we have the technology available to inform ourselves as never before, we are simultaneously and compellingly confronted with the impossibility of ever being fully informed. Even more disturbingly, we are confronted with this impossibility at the very moment when we are told that being informed is more important than ever before to our livelihood, our security, and our social lives.'

Mark Andrejevic[1]

Many of us, I imagine, would agree with the observation that among the most dramatic cultural, social and political changes we have seen over the last two decades is how we access news and information. What has happened in this space has had a transformative effect on our everyday lives.

As the era of mass media gave way to the era of the digital, we had to learn how to deal with a proliferation of online and offline sources through an expanding array of new technologies and mobile devices. While in many respects these changes have been enabling and liberating, they have also led to what looms as a serious existential issue for Western democracies and national polities. It is widely held that we face a crisis in information consequent upon the rearrangement of the media landscape in the digital era. Once, that landscape was dominated by the mass media – and this was, at least in theory, shared by and accessible to the whole population. That has comprehensively changed. Now, for instance, most of our television is delivered only to the subscribers of streaming services; the development of online platforms has opened up niche media sites for targeted audiences, specialised interests and social networks; and the news is disseminated more widely via Facebook and Twitter than by the traditional outlets such as newspapers and television broadcasters. Instead of a media diet composed through our selections from a shared but limited menu, the range of options now available for our individual selection is virtually infinite. There may well be an end to them, but none of us is ever going to reach it.

Why is this seen as a crisis? On the one hand, it might seem like a brave new world of opportunity, with the expansion of possibility promising to enrich our daily lives. However, certain attributes of this new world have emerged as potential challenges to the community's capacity to access the sources of the information they need. The elements which have raised concern include the unmanageable volume of the information available; the ever-increasing circulation of misinformation, disinformation and 'fake news'; the concentration of control of the world of information within the unaccountable hands of the global tech giants such as Meta and Google; the undermining of the integrity of the very idea of news; and the pervasive influence of Big Tech's commercially structured algorithms, which increasingly determine how consumers deal with the 'burden of choice'[2] as they navigate their way through the online sea of news, information and social networks.

While this is a global crisis which has been built upon the dominance of Google, Meta and Apple, and upon their commercial colonisation of the unregulated spaces of the online environment, there is also a story to tell about its specific application to and consequences for Australia. Australia's own news and information infrastructure, as well as how our media's treatment of news, information and expertise has evolved over time, all play their part in shaping the form and the function of Australia's public sphere.

The transformation of news in the digital era

The successful functioning of a modern democracy depends upon its citizens' universal access to accurate information. Traditionally, the function of journalism in providing news and information services has been regarded as a fundamental component of that process.[3] Accordingly, over the mass media era, how news was reported and presented within the traditional media largely respected conventions of objectivity and accuracy, which 'set the boundaries for what counted as mainstream perspectives', as Mark Andrejevic puts it.[4] There was a limited set of sources through which the public could access their news and information, and so there was a reasonable consensus on what these mainstream perspectives included.

For some observers, however, the prevailing structures of ownership and control within our mass media systems raised legitimate concerns that they concentrated power into the hands of too few – indeed, in Australia's case over time, very few – and thus prevented a more diverse range of voices from being heard. This has long been regarded as compromising the quality of our democracy. For those who made such criticisms (and I have been among them myself), the arrival of the digital era brought with it the technical capacity to dramatically increase diversity. Consequently, it held out the promise of greater participation in the production and circulation of information and opinion to those who had hitherto been only consumers. The audience, it seemed, was taking over the stage. Consequently, there was considerable enthusiasm for the changes the digital era offered.

Initially, the early enterprises that emerged to take up the promise of the digital were applauded as a form of 'cool capitalism'.[5] Nobody really saw anything in them that looked like it might threaten the social fabric. Indeed, the digital pioneers in San Francisco created what looked like hip cottage industries, their artisanal/nerdy vibe building on their connection to a history derived from 1960s and 1970s communitarian counterculture.[6] Their objective of building 'connectedness' was initially focused on quite localised communities (Facebook's frat-boy origins as a social network for about 1000 students at Harvard is among the examples of this). So, even as these enterprises were getting up to speed during the 1990s and 2000s, few could have foreseen a future where they would become the global behemoths we know today. And, of course, as their technologies magically connected us not only to each other but also to a world of information and entertainment that had previously been out of reach, all of this seemed to place these technologies and their entrepreneurs on the side of the consumer. So much of what they offered was free, so much of it responded pleasingly to the user's demands, and so much of it was explicitly committed to giving 'power to the people'.

As the online environment has evolved, however, that's not really how it has turned out. Harvard law professor Shoshana Zuboff ruefully recalls the 'illusion' that 'being "connected" is somehow intrinsically pro-social, innately inclusive, or naturally tending toward the democratization of knowledge'. We have learned that while such capacities are certainly there, they are not the only ones. They can also support uses which are not at all pro-social or democratic. Furthermore, as we have seen as the more entrepreneurial business models have evolved, the pro-social development of digital connection within communities can easily be appropriated for the service of these entrepreneurs' commercial ends.[7] Notoriously, the performance of Google and Facebook has demonstrated that these commercial ends have, even when challenged, prevailed over all other considerations.

The conditions which enabled much of this were building for some time. The media environment into which the digital intervened in the 1990s was already well on its way through a period of reinvention and reconfiguration. What is now often called the 'legacy' media (print and broadcast mass media) had been gradually shape-shifting from the 1980s onwards as a consequence of the expansion of the commercial multi-channel market in subscription television (in Australia, pay TV); the free-market enthusiasm in many jurisdictions for the relaxation of limitations on the concentration of ownership and control; the contraction in the presence and influence of public broadcasting; and the declining profitability of, in particular, print news media.

What counted as 'news' was changing as well. In Australia, as the competition for media audiences increased, the rise in 'celebrity news' coverage took off first in the mass-market women's magazines during the 1980s and accelerated into the early 2000s, permeating print outlets across the board – from the mass-market tabloid newspapers to the high-end 'quality' broadsheets. More generally, and across print, radio and television, the content of news services was turning towards entertainment and opinion, and away from traditional news and factual reporting. This had the effect of blurring the conventional distinction between information and entertainment, and challenging the hitherto standard assumptions about the core informational function of the news media.[8]

It is tempting to say that it was all downhill from there. With the rapid emergence of the competing media services, social media platforms and consumer devices that came with the digital, the battle for the audience's attention intensified. Online providers, for their part, were untrammelled by the mass media's ethical or regulatory constraints on accuracy and objectivity, or even by the conventional codes of practice determining what journalism could legitimately do. Consequently, they were able to dress up their content in the livery of 'news', copying news formats and modes of presentation, while populating their sites with all kinds of material – gossip, rumour, 'fake news', 'citizen journalism', user-generated videos, blogs, newsletters, political propaganda and more. It was increasingly difficult for traditional news reporting to compete with this. Eventually, the media and information sector learned that the most effective and immediate way to maximise their audiences' attention and engagement was to frighten them or to make them angry. As a result, the generation of fear and anger, regardless of their potential for inciting hatred and abuse, became a major strategy for many online platforms, as well as for some traditional media outlets. (It was not such a stretch for the print tabloids.)

In this battle for attention, truth has been among the major casualties. The decline in the authority and influence of the traditional providers of news weakened the purchase of the boundaries to mainstream perspectives to which Andrejevic refers. The social contract on what constituted 'the truth' gradually eroded. Conventional understandings gave way to American television comedian Stephen Colbert's tongue-in-cheek coinage of 'truthiness' (that something is true if it 'feels' true), and then, ultimately and extraordinarily, to Trump spokesperson Kellyanne Conway's 'alternative facts' (that it is true if I say it is). The development of the search engines, from Netscape to Google, might have served as a corrective to this, but they provided information on such a scale, and with so little guide to its legitimacy, and so little content moderation, that the welter of information quickly outstripped consumers' ability to assess its accuracy, provenance or purpose.

Of course, much of what is most reliable about this information is still derived from the legacy news media, but this is precisely where investment in the independent production of news and information has been contracting. The supply of new and accurate information from such sources is therefore dwindling. At the same time, the projected capacity for 'search' (that is, Google and other search engines) to compensate for the shift from news to entertainment by generating additional sources of credible news and information has turned out to be quite limited. Search retrieves, aggregates, curates and manages information; by and large, and notwithstanding its promises to do otherwise, it actually does relatively little to produce it.[9]

Social media has inserted itself into this gap, but that has only raised another raft of concerns. While acknowledging the various benefits which have come from the expansion of social media, it is also clear that many social media networks have happily shared false information at scale. Their activity has contributed significantly to the erosion of shared points of truth, to the commodification of rumour and to the provisionalisation of facts. Meanwhile, the massive global networks built by Google and Meta have amplified the volume and extended the reach of misinformation and disinformation, as they have used their algorithms to target their messages ever more specifically to individual subscribers. Under their influence, the ecosystem of news and information has been polluted by fake news, misinformation and disinformation.[10]

'We create our own reality'

This didn't begin, though, with the internet and social media. American journalist Evan Osnos has demonstrated that what he calls 'the contempt for fact' has quite a history in the United States, and has long been evident in the tactics used by powerful organisations seeking to influence public opinion in their favour. He cites a memo from way back in 1969 that was circulated among executives at the Brown and Williamson tobacco company, which suggested how they might use disinformation to combat the threat of increasingly strict regulations on their industry. 'Doubt is our product', it stated, since it is 'the best means of competing with the "body of fact" that exists in the minds of the general public'. Osnos then quotes an aide to President George W. Bush, who in 2004 dismissed criticism from what he called the 'reality-based community'. 'We're an empire now,' the aide told the journalist Ron Suskind, 'and when we act, we create our own reality.'[11]

These are deep roots, then, and Osnos digs them up to remind us that much of this manipulation of 'reality' is deliberately malign, harnessed and put to work in the service of special interests and political or commercial objectives. The success of such a program is evident in what might be considered the shrinkage of the 'reality-based community', both in the United States and in Australia today. In Australia, concern about the significant rise of misinformation and disinformation featured in political commentary on both the 2016 and 2019 federal elections. It became even more prominent and disturbing during the pandemic when health authorities attempted to contest the spread of false information about Covid-19, as well as the viral influence of 'alt-right' conspiracy theories implicated in some of the libertarian protests against community lockdowns and the distribution of vaccines.

Recently, Ed Coper has contextualised the Australian experience within this larger pattern of global development. For him, 'disinformation is a mere symptom of larger forces at work, including an erosion of trust, a fracturing of understanding and a fragmentation of realities'. No longer gathering in a 'shared town square', we 'are losing our common points of reference and our collective sites of memory'. Coper claims that we are now 'rediscovering an ancient era of hostile tribes with frighteningly modern means of information warfare, all with a callous disregard for common purpose and progress'.[12]

It took a little time for these 'larger forces' to emerge. As Coper points out, 'progressives' initially had the 'top hand in online politics, engaging and mobilising freely by embracing these liberating technologies'. This was the promise of digital democratisation bearing fruit, it seemed. Conservatives were slow to engage with the online environment, Coper asserts, but then something changed as the online environment commercialised.[13] Hope and change began to lose the battle against hate and fear, and more extreme, alt-right points of view grew in prominence.[14] Their proponents began to understand the capacities of the network platforms to disseminate and to normalise their views, and thus to recruit followers. Some of these social networks began to work more like closed communities, narrowing their horizons to focus more intently on the interests they pursued.

This may explain why the violent demonstrations against Covid-19 restrictions in Melbourne in 2021 were so puzzling to many observers at the time. 'Where has this come from?' they wondered. Most, at the time, had no knowledge of the networks that were spreading extremist disinformation, and little awareness of their activity in recruiting followers.

We have reached a point when the political implications for our democracy of this aspect of the operation of these social networks are substantial. There is genuine concern across society about how to address them. Appealing to the technology giants' sense of social responsibility for a greater commitment to content moderation has proven a waste of time. While we find ourselves in a world that is increasingly structured and shaped by the power of a handful of global corporations, the interests of these companies are thoroughly commercial.[15] They have demonstrated that they don't much care which way the politics within their various markets go, as long as they are able to maintain their business models, their subscribers and their profits. In fact, they are the perfect expressions of the neoliberal enterprise we discussed in the previous chapter. They are all about maximising profit while expanding their global footprint, and they have proven determinedly opposed to accepting any form of public or civic accountability that might limit their commercial activities.

The power of these organisations is a serious problem, then, for countries such as Australia, which is seeking ways to unilaterally regulate the platforms so that, at the very least, their online behaviours are more closely aligned with the accepted social norms of our offline world. This is what communications researcher José van Dijck and her co-authors describe as a battle between 'private interests and public values'.[16]

This task is further complicated by the fact that so much of what the tech giants actually do is hidden from us. We don't know how their algorithms actually work, to what ends and in whose interests (although we can certainly guess!). Nor do we know how their individually targeted 'dark' advertising impacts people's behaviours and opinions.[17]

Facebook is currently the platform most in the spotlight in this regard. This is not surprising, given Facebook's importance in shaping our contemporary information ecology, and the power it possesses to decide what is allowed to take root and grow within that ecology.[18] That power is being abused. For instance, we are beginning to see the unregulated ways in which Facebook's advertising platform is used in political campaigning, and there is reason to be alarmed at what that might mean for election results, public debates and the spread of misinformation and disinformation.[19] Furthermore, there is now overwhelming evidence that Facebook's algorithms have been (probably deliberately, but certainly irresponsibly) stoking social division and political polarisation. Former Facebook employee and whistleblower Frances Haugen, in her 2021 testimony to the United States Congress, has seen to that.

Facebook, however, has chosen to do as little as possible to correct this situation, because to do otherwise would compromise its business model. It is still sticking to its claims that Facebook's mission is to make the world 'more open and connected', even as it becomes more evident that it is actually contributing significantly towards making the world 'more closed and divided'.[20] Consequently, there is a growing public backlash against Meta's corporate hypocrisy, its privileging of profits over social responsibility, and the disingenuousness of its invocation of a principled libertarian resistance to more active content moderation.[21]

One of the most succinct summative diagnoses of what has gone wrong here comes from Shoshana Zuboff. These tech companies, she says, 'quickly realized that they could do anything they wanted, and they did':

They dressed in the fashions of advocacy and emancipation, appealing to and exploiting contemporary anxieties, while the real action was hidden offstage. Theirs was an invisibility cloak woven in equal measure to the rhetoric of the empowering web, the ability to move swiftly, the confidence of vast revenue streams, and the wild, undefended nature of the territory they would conquer and claim. They were protected by the inherent illegibility of the automated processes that they rule, the ignorance that these processes breed, and the sense of inevitability that they foster.[22]

The failed promise of digital democracy

Not everyone would accept that diagnosis, admittedly, and it has certainly taken a while for that kind of critique to emerge within academic accounts of the digital revolution. Initially, as noted earlier, most academic researchers backed up the industry's enthusiasm for the promise of digital democracy. There was a strongly supportive body of research into the possibilities of new forms of journalism (such as 'citizen journalism'), and the capacities for user-generated content to radically change how the media worked, and in whose interests. The 'digital optimists' championed the internet's democratising potential and the new avenues of public participation made available to ordinary people.[23]

There was considerable enthusiasm, for instance, for how user-generated video content, such as that produced and circulated through YouTube, might subvert the existing power structures within the entertainment industries. The success of independent video producers, operating much like an old-school 'garage band' in producing their short movies and taking them directly to their market, encouraged that kind of enthusiasm.

To some extent, this enthusiasm has been maintained as

independent producers of social media entertainment have continued to bypass the standard gatekeepers for the production and distribution of media content.[24] But the progressive hope that the world of legitimate news and information would expand and diversify as a result of digital media has not been fulfilled.

While I understand the arguments made by researchers such as Brian McNair and his colleagues, their claim that the simple multiplication in the number of 'news' outlets online has made up for other deficiencies that have actually shrunk the informational capacities of the sector is simply not convincing.[25] When you assess the quality of the information now flooding the digital environment and consider the dangers inherent in the degree of corporate concentration online, and when you can see how the proliferation in the number and diversity of sites has been accompanied by the dramatic rise in the circulation of misinformation and disinformation, it is hard to be sanguine about how this will play out in future.

In the United States, social media's intervention into the online ecology of news and information became prominent earlier than in most other markets. This generated criticism which focused on the quality and provenance of the information, and the manner in which it was being discovered, consumed and shared. Legal scholar Cass Sunstein's work was particularly influential: he pointed to the danger created by the diminution of a mainstream media presence which operated as a point of truth for the society.[26] What was developing in its place, Sunstein argued, was a multiplicity of relatively self-contained sites which filtered out alternative points of view in order to more effectively promote their own. It was suggested that these 'filter bubbles' separated users from the wider community, while promulgating often misinformed, misleading or deliberately disruptive views of the world.[27] As users increasingly stayed with their favoured news sites, encountering only views with which they already agreed, there was a danger of what Sunstein called 'cyber-balkanisation' – the political fragmentation of the online community. What was often also described as 'confirmation bias' was thought to encourage the public to stay away from any news and information that challenged their existing beliefs or opinions.

While his 2013 book *Infoglut* was largely supportive of Sunstein's analysis, cultural studies and media theorist Mark Andrejevic's most recent book, *Automated Media*, expresses reservations about the idea that this is primarily a matter of the range and variety of the information that is consumed:

> It has become exceedingly clear in recent years that mere exposure to a wide range of perspectives does little to promote openness or curiosity on the part of those who view debate simply as an opportunity to score a win for their ideological position and countervailing facts as something to be suppressed, misconstrued, or simply denied. Much of what passes for discussion and debate online provides a ready refutation of the notion that access to a greater range of information and perspectives creates a better-informed citizenry.[28]

This is not just the fault of the internet, Andrejevic points out, as 'cable news' (such as Fox News in the United States and Sky News in Australia) is equally culpable for its efforts in recasting 'public debate as a latter-day Punch and Judy show featuring increasingly extreme characters'.[29] The social and cultural fragmentation we see reflected online and in news/opinion sites such as these has coincided with what Andrejevic describes as a 'political assault on the conditions that enable citizens to take into consideration the needs, perspectives, and values of others, including those whom they do not know and may never meet but who nevertheless form part of their shared communities'.[30]

Andrejevic cites research which has found that people who are exposed to a broader range of information may nonetheless appear to be 'less inclined to take into consideration the larger community of which they are part and the perspectives of those unknown others who comprise it'.[31] If this is indeed the case, it points to a fundamental fracturing of our sense of community. Andrejevic suggests, as do some other researchers, that the resistance to countervailing facts and opinions may not be simply a consequence of filter bubbles or 'echo chambering' – only hearing opinions with which they agree. Rather, it may be due to 'the degradation of people's ability to see themselves as part of an imagined community in which the concerns and interests of others, both individually and collectively, matter'.[32] What Andrejevic claims is lacking in these people's world view is technology activist Eli Pariser's notion of a 'civic disposition': the 'willingness to act on behalf of the public good while being attentive to and considerate of the feelings, needs, and attitudes of others'.[33]

Automating culture

But wait – that's not all. Before leaving this topic, let's look briefly at one further cause for concern. This relates not only to the content of the messages we receive, or the social context in which we understand them, but also how we encounter them.[34]

There has been a substantial and significant shift in this area of our experience. The problem of how each of us navigates our way through the infinite possibilities of the online information environment is no longer a personal one. Rather, we have accommodated ourselves to the idea that making the many choices required has become a burden best relieved by automated technologies. These manage the algorithms which generate the selection of news items that turn up when we search for something using Google or open our Facebook newsfeed, even the 'recommendations' that appear when we open Netflix.[35] We might happily accept the recommendations generated by our online providers, but we don't necessarily recognise that this allows them to access the personal data our acceptance generates.

This is symptomatic of how our ambivalent relation to the online environment has developed over time. Most of us seem to have accepted (perhaps not consciously) that this is an engagement which offers us a form of empowerment, on the one hand, while simultaneously exploiting us by invisibly mining, and then commercially trading, the data generated by our response to its attractions, on the other.[36] In what may seem a reasonable trade-off, we outsource our selection of information to an automated system that is impenetrable and almost ubiquitous, which seems to 'understand' us and to be working in our interests, but which is also nudging us in the directions most likely to generate commercial benefits for the organisation running the system.

This amounts to the commercial automation of everyday life – indeed, of the production of culture. We may be comfortable thinking of automation only as something which is about replacing human workers with electronically operated machines – in contexts such as the manufacturing or resources industries, for instance, or in the retail websites we use to purchase products and commodities. But automation is far more pervasive than that, and figures ever more significantly in what we might think of as routine personal activities in our everyday lives.[37] So, when an algorithm decides what items to feature in your social media newsfeed or what video you should stream next, or what ad you are most likely to respond to, that's automation.[38] The economic benefits of the supposed efficiencies are what drives the commercial take-up of automation and artificial intelligence, but there is a growing body of argument and research that strongly advises caution, given the likely social, cultural and political implications of the spread of these technologies in the future.[39]

There is a growing body of research that attempts to understand how the algorithms which drive automated media work and what their social consequences are. Jonathan Cohn notes that there are now many humanities scholars (that is, not computer scientists) considering the larger role algorithms play in shaping our culture, economy, politics and everyday reality.[40] The recurring concern is that the operation of commercial, political and administrative customisation through the technologies of automation, no matter what principles were embedded in their initial design, may in practice be detrimental to the social and political fabric.

Most notably, what Virginia Eubanks has labelled 'the automation of inequality' has been increasingly highlighted as a problem governments need to understand before increasing their investment in the application of such technologies. She notes, for instance, the role of automation in government online forms accessed by individuals seeking services, applying for jobs, establishing eligibility and so on, which can serve to amplify the disadvantages experienced by those community members who do not easily fit the standard requirements of the form (for instance, those with no driver's licence or passport for identification purposes).

Eubanks examines, in the US context, what happens when automated systems are used to make social, political and judicial decisions that have complex, often unforeseen, human consequences for those who are their subjects. These could include decisions about 'which neighborhoods get policed, which families attain needed resources, who is short-listed for employment, and who is investigated for fraud'.[41]

In summary, Eubanks claims, 'automated decision-making shatters the social safety net, criminalizes the poor, intensifies discrimination and compromises our deepest national values'.[42] If that seems a little overstated, it is worth thinking for a moment about how well such a description fits some of the most egregious examples from Australia, such as the unlawful rollout of Robodebt by the federal government from 2015 to 2020, or the botched and discriminatory automation of the entitlement assessment process for the NDIS during 2021.[43]

News and information in Australia

How has all of this played out in Australia? If one were to search for the most popular sources of news in Australia, the results would show that ABC TV and the commercial television networks Seven, Nine and Ten dominate, with News.com.au and the online Australian edition of *The Guardian* scoring highly as well.

On the one hand, such results might comfort those who worry about the provision of news being taken out of the hands of traditional news organisations and their journalists. On the other hand, it might concern those who had hoped that the market dominance of these organisations in Australia might begin to decline under the pressure of online competition. Australia is still one of the most concentrated media markets in the world, with one global study ranking Australia's newspaper ownership as the third-most concentrated in the world, after only China and Egypt.[44] Rupert Murdoch's News Corp's control of Australia's print media – almost 70 per cent of the metropolitan markets – has long been an issue of public debate, not only due to the intensity of its concentration but also due to the partisan performance of its newspapers, and their penchant for mounting campaigns against those they deem to be their enemies.[45]

News Corp's dominance of the local and regional newspaper market has been of particular concern in recent times as well, as the company has closed down the print editions of literally hundreds of local newspapers, moving them online, where they sit behind a metropolitan newspaper paywall, destined to be abandoned when locals decline to pay for a product that is inferior to the one they used to get, in some cases, for free.

There are further challenges for the Australian news media to consider here. There are far fewer journalists, for a start. While there have been significant corporate mergers aimed at creating economies of scale (such as that involving the Nine Network and Fairfax newspapers), this has not been focused on protecting jobs. In 2020 alone, Australia lost more than 2000 newsroom and related roles,[46] compounding what the Media, Entertainment and Arts Alliance (MEAA) has estimated to be between 4000 and 5000 journalism jobs lost over the past decade.[47] Those who remain face the task of reporting across multiple formats (in some cases, doing versions of the same story for radio, television, print and online), and continually updating stories online, in addition to meeting established print or broadcast deadlines. This means that our journalists must even more ruthlessly prioritise what they cover, for how long and in what detail.

There are fewer opportunities now for investigative journalism, as the profit margins, especially in print, leave little room for the substantial time investment such work requires. Many more journalists are freelancers, their conditions of employment precarious. The ABC and SBS try to maintain their level of public information services, but budget cuts have significantly impacted the scale and quality of the ABC's news and current affairs, for instance, resulting in the cutting of key programs (such as the Friday edition of television's *7.30*) and the closure of some of its foreign news bureaus. The long-term trend in commercial television news and current affairs towards abandoning the coverage of politics and policy has continued, as the market logic of entertainment prevails.[48]

Implicated in all of this are the shifts in the national patterns of news consumption: in 2021 only 4 per cent of the population had a newspaper or magazine subscription, while 54 per cent of Generation Z (14–24 years old), 41 per cent of Millennials (25–38) and 27 per cent of Generation X (39–55) cited social media as their favoured source of news.[49] A generational divide is opening up between those under the age of fifty-five and those who are older in how they source their news, with the older demographics still preferring traditional news media.[50]

Ed Coper points to another issue, however, which is to do with a particular aspect of the growth in the dissemination of news and information in Australia, and which highlights the influence of Sky News, social networks and prominent purveyors of disinformation such as Clive Palmer and Craig Kelly. Coper examines the degree to which this influence is based on the sharing of news and information via social networks (retweeting on Twitter, for instance, or sharing among friends on Facebook). Sharing, when done at scale, can effectively turn rumour, misinformation or even straight-out falsehood into news. For example, a rumour posted by one person may be shared among a small group of 'friends' initially, but if it attracts sufficient attention from them, the sharing extends further. As a result, and as the circulation expands, what may have started out as rumour can begin to operate as if it were fact. The volume of the traffic around a particular post or topic builds its credibility and its power to influence opinion and generate further postings. Enough volume and enough attention, and a post becomes news.

Hence the proliferation of fake accounts delivering targeted disinformation and the deployment of 'bots' (automated accounts sending out, potentially, thousands of messages) to raise the profile of a particular posting to the level of the 'viral'.

According to Coper, the Australian news media's reporting on social media trends reflects a poor understanding of this process, paying attention only to the most 'visited' news sites (currently, the ABC records the highest number of visitors). This overlooks the important factor of how widely news stories are shared and circulated on social networks. Media reports may mock Sky News for only picking up 3 per cent of the television audience but they miss the fact that it is Australia's most shared news site. It is also the number one news site on YouTube, and the most engaged-with Australian media brand on Facebook. Facebook posts from Sky in 2020, Coper reports, had 'more shares than the ABC News, SBS News, 7News Australia, 9News and 10News First Pages put together. Sky News videos on their Australian YouTube channel have been viewed more than *a billion* times – double the amount of ABC News total views.' The fact that Sky News is now 'firmly implanted in the digital ecosystem of the right wing culture wars' (that is, within the world of misinformation that thrives online), says Coper, has gone 'largely unnoticed as most media observers have yet to catch up with a non-traditional media landscape'.[51]

The mainstream media's treatment of news has come to favour opinion over information as a means of attracting audiences, but social media has taken this one step further. On social media, opinion can effectively pass for information. The power of these opinions is not to be underestimated. Social media activity is often treated in other media reports as if it accurately reflects actual shifts in public opinion (the common 'what's trending on social media now' segments). This may constitute an overstatement or even a misrepresentation of its significance, and a misunderstanding of what is actually generating that activity (it could simply be hundreds of fake accounts, for instance). Perversely, such reporting works to magnify the impression of social media's influence as if it represents an authentic 'finger on the pulse' of the community and their attitudes, rather than what may simply be a 'bunch of angry tweets'.[52]

Unfortunately, such overstatement of social media's significance may well be feeding into the tendency evident in other sectors of the media to modify their practices and their content to be more 'successful' online. This, one could argue, has contributed to the development of a more opinionated, less evidence-based and less civil media environment overall.

And so this, then, is where we find ourselves in Australia, at a time when crucial policy and strategic decisions are up in the air, waiting for a community consensus to assert itself or for courageous political leadership to chart a positive direction into the future.

A community in need of accurate and useful information finds itself swamped by information that may or may not be accurate or useful, but which is delivered at such scale that we are ill-equipped to make those kinds of distinctions. The Big Tech companies have brought in their machines to 'help', providing us with automated recommendations for things we might like to know or consume. Along the way, they have intervened in the production of culture by nudging our choices in the direction of profitable outcomes for their organisation. Operating at scale, relentless, ubiquitous and targeted, these machines are tuning the culture to particular wavelengths, and this inevitably has sociocultural and political consequences. At the same time, social media networks have opened up a domain of communication that is turning out to be as divisive and antisocial as it has been socially connective.

This crisis of information is a symptom of an accelerating

revolution in the making of culture, a revolution in which the interests of the nation and of the citizen are likely to be set aside unless significant action is taken to defend them.

The attack on knowledge

There are treatments available for this condition. Central among them is the generation, sharing and diffusion of knowledge: the 'public good par excellence'.[53] Unfortunately, in Australia over recent years, knowledge and expertise have come under sustained ideological attack. As they have increasingly butted up against the politics of the day, they have been dismissed as the property and privilege of the 'elites', or as the tool of activists and special interests, rather than as something that should be valued as a national asset and a common good.

Tom Nichols' widely noted *The Death of Expertise: The campaign against established knowledge and why it matters* describes the situation in the United States, where he claims that while expertise isn't dead, 'it's in trouble'. 'Something is going terribly wrong,' Nichols writes. 'The United States is now a country obsessed with the worship of its own ignorance.'[54] In an attempt to understand why Americans appear in fact to be '*proud* of not knowing things', he suggests that rejecting the advice of experts has become a way of asserting personal autonomy, 'a way for Americans to insulate their increasingly fragile egos from ever being told they're wrong about anything'.[55]

Not one to hold back his judgements, Nichols asserts that 'the foundational knowledge of the average American is now so low it has crashed through the floor of "uninformed", passed "misinformed" on the way down, and is now plummeting to "aggressively wrong"'.[56] Furthermore, he finds it particularly striking that this dismissal of expertise is not only delivered with such frequency and on so many issues, but that it is accompanied by so much anger:

> [I]t may be that attacks on expertise are more obvious due to the ubiquity of the Internet, the undisciplined nature of the conversation on social media, or the demands of the twenty-four-hour news cycle. But there is a self-righteousness and fury to this new rejection of expertise that suggest, at least to me, that this isn't just mistrust or questioning or the pursuit of alternatives: it is narcissism, coupled to a disdain for expertise as some sort of exercise in self-actualization.[57]

This has echoes of the 'American fury' that Evan Osnos documents in *Wildland*, and its antisocial narcissism also chimes with the decline in the civic disposition and the corresponding rise in the models of self-interested individualism that are at the heart of the neoliberal subjectivity.

Nichols' critique of this situation comes from a peculiarly American conservative politics, so there are limits to how readily one might translate his analysis to the Australian context. A specific element of the context Nichols addresses, of course, is Donald Trump, the 'one-man campaign against established knowledge'.[58] Australia hasn't yet come up with leaders with quite Trump's record of disdain for knowledge and disregard for the truth, but Scott Morrison certainly comes into contention. Another former prime minister, Tony Abbott, has form in this territory as well, once notoriously dismissing the science on climate change as 'absolute crap'.[59]

More importantly, however, and over the period on which we have been focusing, Australian governments have acted in ways that have not only directly impacted on Australia's capacity to generate knowledge that is in the public interest, but in some cases they have removed or impeded public access to knowledge that has already been created. There is a long list of government-funded research bodies that have been targeted in recent years, particularly those charged with providing advice on how to prepare communities to respond to climate change. After Abbott won office in 2013, he defunded the Climate Change Adaptation Flagship at CSIRO, the National Climate Change Adaptation Research Facility at Griffith University, and the Climate Commission, an independent body created by the federal government in 2011. The treatment of the Climate Commission was especially vindictive, with its head, Tim Flannery, sacked via a telephone call within hours of the Abbott government being elected; the research it had posted on its website was subsequently removed.[60]

Less noticed by the media and the public, but in my view significant, was the abolition of the Prime Minister's Science, Engineering and Innovation Council (PMSEIC), an independent foresighting committee of experts set up to provide medium- to long-term evidence-based advice to government on the national interest. PMSEIC was established in the 1990s and usefully served administrations of both colours until it was replaced by the more politically oriented Science Council after Abbott became prime minister.[61] (Interestingly, in 2009 PMSEIC provided an expert report to the federal parliament on the SARS epidemic, which focused on how to devise a response to a potential pandemic; one wonders how much difference PMSEIC might have made if it had still been in place when the Covid-19 pandemic began.)

There were numerous occasions during the Abbott/Turnbull/ Morrison era when the government not only publicly rejected important expert advice, but refused even to meet with those best able to provide it. It was widely reported that the group of former disaster and emergency response officials led by Greg Mullins, a former commissioner of Fire and Rescue New South Wales, sought meetings with Morrison well before the Black Summer bushfires in 2019 to warn of the impending danger, and during 2021 before the floods which followed. The expert group's repeated attempts to put their case for preventive action directly to the prime minister were rejected, and the consequences have been there for all to see over the last three years.

There is also, of course, a long list of royal commissions (into the banking industries, childcare, aged care, disability services, sexual harassment in the workplace and more), as well as a number of Productivity Commission inquiries, whose evidence, advice and recommendations have been ignored, set aside or rejected. Even when some recommendations have been implemented, as occurred after the Royal Commission into Misconduct in the Banking, Superannuation and Financial Services Industry, they were walked back as soon as changed circumstances allowed. A number of the consumer protections established for the banking and finance industries in the wake of that royal commission were rescinded during the pandemic, for instance.

In so many cases over this period, experts have been cast as enemies of the public, important information has been filtered through the pragmatics of politics, and knowledge has been treated with contempt.

The costs of such a pattern of behaviour are best revealed by a contrary example: the straightforward manner in which federal and state governments drew upon scientific and medical expertise to provide the community with important information during the first phase of the Covid pandemic. Putting forward the chief medical officers as authoritative spokespersons during 2020 was a key mechanism for building the trust and cooperation that marked the Australian response to the first wave of deaths and hospitalisations, as testing and isolation protocols were instituted. While there was some public friction between experts over their media performances (especially between the professional epidemiologists and the media's most influential health correspondent, the ABC's Dr Norman Swan[62]), there was generally a confluence of views as politicians honestly relayed the advice they had been given. (If only, many said, a similar level of respect could be shown to our climate scientists!)

However, as the urgency drained out of the situation, especially during the temporary lull before the arrival of the Delta variant, the politicians hit the switch back to ideology, the chief medical officers were no longer put before the media, and a cocktail of mixed messages on vaccines, treatments and lockdowns was generated. By the time Australia was being swamped by Omicron in 2021, much of the trust that had been built between our state and federal politicians and the public had been weakened. The community response to the public health advice followed suit. It was a revealing, if inadvertent, experiment in just how an evidence-led, pro-social government information project could work, if properly and honestly managed in the public interest.

This remains, however, something of an exception, certainly for those politicians who have sought to undermine expert advice in their areas of interest if it does not accord with their preferred ideological or political settings. In their 2021 book on the Morrison government, Wayne Errington and Peter van Onselen discuss how politicised this war on expertise has become, sheeting at least part of it home to 'right-wing polemicists' who might think they are 'strategically clever to discredit experts they don't agree with by using a populist label to paint them as out of touch'.[63] The 'railing against "elites"', they note, has significantly negative consequences for the community, driving a more general distrust of those who represent established knowledge.

This may be slightly overstated, given Mark Evans' research, which finds that experts are still trusted far more than politicians, but it is certainly implicated in the online exhortations for people to 'do their own research' rather than trust established sources.[64]

While Errington and Van Onselen clearly emphasise how fundamental the respect for knowledge is to the functioning of a modern society, they also express some sympathy with Nichols' criticism of academics and universities in the United States, the claim being that they have compromised their standing by pursuing activism rather than scholarship.[65] The situation in Australia is very different, in my view, not only because of how universities developed here, but also because the public engagement of academics in Australia has actually shrunk significantly over time. To some extent this is to do with the manner in which politicians and the media have treated them – I am thinking not just of the disrespect scholars encounter in their personal interactions, but also of the abusive pushback they often receive on social media. As a consequence, Errington and Van Onselen observe, 'more and more academics are retreating from public debates, talking instead only to one another in scholarly journals read by very few people'.[66]

What is most regrettable about the attack on established knowledge in Australia is that so much of it has been focused upon running down the national institutions which produce knowledge, such as the universities and the public broadcasters. Presumably, this is because these institutions are not only sources of knowledge but also of alternative, and potentially critical, points of view. Regarded as competing with government for authority in the public sphere, the universities have been the target of Australia's residual anti-intellectualism – which is always there to be revived, even when apparently dormant, in the service of political interests. There remains a reservoir of popular resentment of the institutions of higher learning – easily caricatured as 'ivory towers' and sites of privilege – that can be exploited when the need arises. A recent example saw Morrison characterising the research-based universities – that is, our most internationally competitive and successful universities – as places where one 'walks around in gowns and looks down on everybody. And, you know, only looks at things that are remotely interesting to anyone.'[67]

The media have, in their own way, contributed to this dynamic by treating experts from time to time as pretenders, or as an irritating challenge to their own cultural authority. It is routine for journalists to use the word 'academic' as a pejorative, a way of dismissing an opinion or concern as irrelevant or unhelpful. My own experience, drawing upon the interviews where I have been 'the expert' myself, suggests that some journalists would really prefer to go it alone on a topic, and resent being required to find an expert who will go on the record to authorise their position. Many academics will recognise the experience of being contacted by a journalist to provide a quote in support of a narrative that is already in place, only to find the journalist loses interest as soon as they say, 'Well, it is a little more complicated than that …'

Notably, Errington and Van Onselen, even while lamenting the decline of expertise, also discuss the role of academics and other experts in a manner that suggests such folk should be careful to stay in their lanes if they are not to be regarded as 'activists' and thus discounted – a line that is a little too close, in my estimation, to the previous government's standard response to any expert who delivered a message they did not welcome.[68]

In fact, journalists too have come under sustained attack as the producers and disseminators of knowledge. The use of federal police to conduct raids upon the homes of political journalists has no place in an open, democratic society, but in the last three years these have occurred on several occasions – prompting accusations that the Australian Federal Police has been politicised. The formal processes involved in, and the official responses to, freedom-of-information (FOI) requests seem to be working in order to frustrate journalists' access to information rather than to facilitate it, while complaints about editorial bias at the ABC – along with veiled threats about its future funding – constitute a deliberate campaign of intimidation.

Indeed, the extent of efforts to intimidate, if not actually silence, Australian journalists has been sufficient to provoke the establishment of an alliance of journalists (the Alliance for Journalists' Freedom) from across the commercial and public service media. Their white paper, titled *Press Freedom in Australia: With light, trust*, set out a seven-point reform agenda for the protection of press freedom in Australia, including a proposal to legislate a wide-ranging 'Media Freedom Act'.[69] A recent report on 'media freedom' from the international organisation Reporters Without Borders had Australia sliding from its previous ranking of twenty-fifth out of 180 countries to thirty-ninth, well behind neighbours New Zealand (eleventh) and Timor-Leste (seventeenth). To explain this slide, the report cites the concentration of media ownership, the tightening of national security laws and the harassment of journalists as combining to 'endanger public-interest journalism in Australia'.[70]

One might be forgiven for thinking that the accumulation of all of this looks slightly sinister. Any autocrat worth their salt would commence a program of social and political control by attacking alternative sources of knowledge and independent expertise. These would be precisely the institutions and professions we have mentioned here: the universities, the public broadcasters and the news media. Put this together with some of the media's criticisms of the tightening of national security and surveillance settings in recent years, and it might suggest that Australia's commitment to the fundamentals of democracy has become patchy.[71]

What is most worrying, as we consider the long-term consequences of the assault on knowledge for Australia, is that in all of these cases, what is on the one hand treated as a threat to government is, on the other hand, clearly a public benefit for the nation: the production, circulation and diffusion of knowledge, the critical scrutiny it informs, and the authority that comes from the disinterested pursuit of the truth.

What has all this to do with the state of the shrinking nation? Quite a bit, in my view. As the pandemic should have taught us, respect for knowledge and expertise is a dangerous value to be setting aside, now more than ever. More broadly, the attack on knowledge diminishes us, cutting us off from a better future. Those who have cynically and irresponsibly prosecuted such attacks for personal, commercial or political interests have put that future at risk. Unfortunately, large sections of the media, for one reason or another, have either been complicit with such attacks or have thoughtlessly enabled them. Reporting (and thus amplifying) ridiculous political attack lines such as 'electric cars will end the weekend' for an attention-grabbing headline, rather than reporting it critically as the nonsense it is (or just not reporting it at all!), is far from the best we should expect from our journalists.

As for the crisis in information, the pollution of our information ecology compromises our ability to manage our everyday lives. It impacts upon our working lives, our personal relationships and our public debate. Unfortunately, it looks as if most of us have given up trying to deal with this. Wearily, we have allowed the algorithms which drive the search engines and social media to manage the bewildering range of choices for us, relinquishing our control over an ever-expanding range of social, cultural and personal activities. At its most pervasive, the spread of automation in these domains outsources the production of culture and erodes our social and political sovereignty. At the same time, it invisibly fine-tunes the construction of personal identities towards the desired commercial outcomes. (The centrality of that objective has even resulted in the creation of a new occupation: the 'influencer'.)

As a consequence of the rise of social media networks, the manner in which our communities are constructed is changing in ways we need to more closely examine and better understand. All of this amounts to a significant reconfiguration of our culture, one that is set to have profound effects on what we know, how we think and, ultimately, what kind of future we inhabit.

What can be done about it? In relation to the attack on knowledge in Australia, this is a matter of political choice and could be halted in a heartbeat. There has to be pressure from the rest of us, including from books like this, to undermine the political confidence that such strategies will be tolerated by the public. Again, the media have an important part to play here, not only because there are some sections of (in particular) the Murdoch press who have been major players in the attack on knowledge, but also because journalists and their editors do have the option of refusing to uncritically relay such content to their readers and viewers. While it is certainly the easier option, the media don't have to serve as publicists for those seeking to mislead the public in order to achieve social, political or commercial advantage. They have a choice, and more of them need to make it in the public interest.

Dealing with the crisis in information is more difficult – even though it is clear that there is widespread and bipartisan political and social concern about the possible consequences of an unregulated online environment for our society. Finding ways to regulate and control participatory media, to better manage the conflict between private interests and public values, is fraught with complications related to free speech and censorship.

Even when such issues are successfully managed, however, the practicalities of regulating social media raise significant difficulties for individual jurisdictions, such as the nation-state. Larger constellations of states, such as the European Union, have managed to exert pressure on Big Tech and achieve some control over their behaviour. Australia has achieved some modest success when undertaking unilateral action – forcing Google and Facebook, for instance, to come to an agreement to pay for some (but not, arguably, enough) of its use of Australian media content. There are other strategies available which might help the state and the citizen to regain some control. More bespoke regulatory structures are being developed in a number of countries, and there are taxation measures which can provide incentives for more pro-social corporate behaviour and responsibility. France and Sweden, for instance, have long operated systems of state-funded subvention to support local and national outlets for public-interest journalism. Around the world, however, countries are continuing to grapple with how to rein in the commercial power, the cultural influence and the social implications of a global operation that reaches directly into the consciousness of their citizens. At this point, there is no clear solution in sight – but there is certainly political interest in seeking one.

In the end, our protection against these potential harms on the one hand, and our capacity to take advantage of the extraordinary possibilities offered within the online environment on the other hand, depend upon the sophistication of our understanding of and knowledge about both of these potentials. There is no doubt that Australia would benefit from better community awareness of why the quality of our information matters.

Furthermore, it is imperative that such an enhanced awareness should be accompanied by a renewed social, cultural and political commitment to defending the importance of truth (rather than 'truthiness'), facts (rather than rumour and opinion) and the centrality of knowledge and expertise to the pursuit of social, cultural and political progress. That is one of the more urgent and important tasks ahead of all of us – not just the media or the political class – as we push back against the shrinking nation.

CHAPTER 5

What's become of the public good?

'[I]f … the economy provides the means which enables us to do the things we consider really important, then we clearly need to begin by having some sense of what is really important and tailor our economic activities accordingly.'

Stefan Collini[1]

What has become of notions of the national interest and the public good within the making of public policy? That is the core question for this chapter. More specifically, it focuses on how the working definition of the national interest has been so narrowed down that it has become overwhelmingly concerned with the state of the economy rather than with the state of the nation. Indeed, even this diminished version of the national interest has been further reduced as it has become most closely identified with the interests and commercial values of the business sector and the resources industries.

Over the last few decades, governments have become much more responsive to the business sector's *projections* of what the economy needs than to public-sector calls to address the *demonstrated* needs of the society or the culture. Appeals to a more traditional conception of the public good – to do with community wellbeing, equality of opportunity, social justice or national cultural development, for instance – have largely been ignored. While the Albanese government's first budget statement explicitly invoked the importance of national 'wellbeing', it is worth remembering how vigorously that idea was derided by the Coalition when Labor was in opposition. And, to be sure, the idea of a 'wellbeing budget', at this point, remains a thought bubble rather than a reality. The status quo still has governments and policy-makers focused on a market-oriented version of the national interest, assessing it primarily in terms of wealth creation and commercial success.[2]

Disturbingly for the future quality of our democracy, the public good is rarely mentioned in the articulation of public policy these days. As Brett Hutchins has noted, the prioritisation of economistic categories such as efficiency, competitiveness and productivity has displaced any sustained attempt to promote the development of a just and equitable society or a distinctive national culture through policy development and implementation.[3] Our experience of the various environmental, social, health and political crises over recent years has revealed just how poorly the nation has been served by these priorities.

This version of the national interest diverges significantly from, for instance, the approach taken by Australian governments during the period immediately following World War II, when they led a broad-based social and cultural program of nation formation.[4] This was not only to do with building things – housing, material infrastructure and so on. It was also to do with building a cohesive national community, a well-resourced civil society and a national culture. Rowe, Turner and Waterton have described this as a commitment to a project of 'nationing'.[5] What has happened in recent years is the antithesis of such a project. Instead, we have what appears to be a deliberate strategy to undermine some of the very institutions which have played fundamental roles in creating our public culture and the vitality of our civil society.

Errington and Van Onselen's account of the Morrison government claims that 'helping mates and punishing enemies is the template for the contemporary Liberal party'. They remind us of the pre-history of the Liberal Party, when it was the United Australia Party (1931–45) and 'widely perceived as the tool of big business'. Errington and Van Onselen describe the contemporary version of the Liberal Party as equally committed to 'mates and corporate chequebooks', and intently focused on settling ideological and cultural scores with sections of Australian society they have long regarded as hostile.[6] Their list of the Liberal Party's enemies includes some of Australia's most important public institutions: the ABC, the universities, the Human Rights Commission, the Australia Council, and much of the arts, heritage and cultural sector. Errington and Van Onselen are not the only ones making this claim. Indeed, there are more targets one could add to this list (such as those charities attacked for undertaking 'advocacy', for instance).[7]

The selection of targets reflects the battlelines drawn up during the culture wars of the 1980s and 1990s. The most disturbing feature of this list, however, is what these organisations and institutions have in common. They all share, in various ways and to a varied extent, the fundamental purpose of serving the public good. Bizarrely, in the diminished and hyper-partisan context of national policy formation in contemporary Australia, it is precisely those institutions most unequivocally committed to serving the public good which have been characterised by successive governments as peripheral to, or even enemies of, the national interest.

What's the good of the public good?

The idea of the public good underpins the establishment of the institutions of a civil society. These institutions provide benefits to the whole of the nation and are deemed to be of sufficient importance that they are worth funding in their own right. British humanities professor Stefan Collini has explained our support for such forms of public provision in the following terms:

> I may choose not to have children, but I am happy to contribute to the costs of maternity hospitals, primary schools, and so on because I want to live in a society that makes civilized provision for these things. I may rarely or never visit various kinds of specialized museums since I am not particularly interested in their contents, but I am happy to contribute to their costs through taxation because I want to live in a society which cares for these things, which does not forget its past, and which recognizes the imaginative and emotional stimulus such objects can provide.[8]

The creation of such institutions reflects what we might think of as the values the public holds in common. Many have their roots in the development of civil society during the nineteenth century – libraries and museums, for instance, but also public schools, universities and systems of social welfare. Others have developed more recently and are focused on objectives such as ensuring the recognition of human rights, preserving the nation's histories, or investing in the maintenance of a confident and vibrant culture through the arts and cultural development.

There is a moral dimension to conceptions of the public good as well, which is about making choices that involve obligations to others, and not just calculations about what's best for ourselves. When members of a society ask, 'What is the right or decent thing to do?' they necessarily draw upon their understandings of these mutual obligations.[9]

Some public goods have obvious material benefits for the whole community – the provision of decent roads and public transport, for instance. However, it is those activities serving the public good that do not appear to provide such evident material benefits to the community which have been most challenged. Where the public good can be measured or quantified or commercialised, there is less of a problem. But where a public good is to do with, for instance, the maintenance of a national cultural identity, or where it performs an educative or civilising function, then it is highly likely, in the current environment, to be cast as an expendable indulgence, catering only to an elite set of interests that are defined as being in opposition to those of the rest of us.

At times, the idea of the public good is articulated slightly differently – such as through the phrase 'the common good'.[10] Both formulations reflect the imperative of promoting general welfare, but their emphasis is slightly different. The power of the fundamental human commitment to the common good has been abundantly evident and, regrettably, desperately needed in Australia over the last couple of years. We have seen it in the heroism of volunteer firefighters who have risked their lives to save threatened rural townships from the Black Summer firestorms, and in the selflessness and bravery of healthcare workers in clinics and hospitals during the pandemic. For many Australians, risking their personal safety for the common good seems to come naturally.

The notion of the public good, however, is more to do with how the nation is managed. It is about how the nation's policies and institutions serve the welfare of its people – and not just their economic interests, but their social, cultural and other fundamental existential needs. This more abstract application of the public good is a little harder for people to discern and acknowledge. This is partly because the benefits underpin civil society implicitly, rather than operating in the foreground of everyday life, and partly because the benefits are themselves expressions of the society's common values, the very things we are most likely to take for granted.

Historically, in most Western democracies, it has fallen to the state and to public institutions to serve as the 'designated custodians' of the public good.[11] They have a special function in this regard in preserving public values and protecting the collective interest in how they are managed. As time has gone by, however, and as the contest between commercial interests and public values has heated up, it has become increasingly difficult for governments, and particularly populist democratic governments, to maintain a balance between these opposing forces. As the terms of the debate have narrowed, and as the principle of commercialisation has dominated so much of public policy, politicians have struggled to find a way of promoting the claims of things which traditionally have been regarded as good in themselves against the claims of what consumers are said to want.[12] Given the length of the electoral cycle, short-term material benefit has the priority over the long-term support of processes aimed at the embedding of common values.

Nonetheless, most would agree, in principle, that one of the most important functions of the democratic state is to preserve the institutions and individual rights of a civil society independently of party political interests, on the one hand, and of the unfettered market economy, on the other.[13] In practice, and especially these days, that is easier said than done.

The ABC and the 'cultural elite'

Government budgets are clear indicators of their priorities, so the allocation of funds over time tells a story. This is why those designing the budget are often reluctant to acknowledge that what they are doing represents an actual shift in priorities. In deflecting such an interpretation, they can cite the unwelcome influence of external factors on their decisions, or perhaps contingent issues to do with the particular condition of the organisation in question.

The convenient principle of future 'sustainability' often turns up here, as if there is some irresistible natural force, rather than politics, driving these decisions. There is also the claim that a budget initiative is about 'changing the culture' of an institution – typically towards one that is more inclined towards strategies of commercialisation. Even something as relatively straightforward as whether the budget of an institution (or, in the case of the universities, a whole sector) has actually been cut becomes a subject of furious debate as each side rolls out its preferred set of figures and statistics.

The fact that this is such contentious political territory should remind us that there is little unintended about the consequences. The treatment of the institutions serving the public good upon which this chapter is focused may be open to various interpretations and assessments as to their actual extent and effect, but any damage they have sustained can hardly be viewed as accidental.

Let us start with the ABC. It is broadly recognised that mounting a full-scale attack on the ABC is politically risky. Regarded by the public as one of the country's most trusted organisations, and still the resource most Australians turn to when an emergency heightens the public's need for accurate and timely information, the ABC has a fundamental place not only in our information and communications infrastructure but also – as the major public broadcaster – within the structure of our democracy.[14] Even though governments of both colours have bristled at the broadcaster's criticism of the party in power, politicians know that there is strong support for public funding of the ABC, and that any openly punitive program of budget cuts could have electoral consequences, especially in rural areas. So there is some caution, even at times stealth, in how cuts to the ABC budget tend to be done: they are usually targeted or incremental rather than swingeing.

There has also been a long-term political investment in challenging the ABC's claims of entitlement. For many years the federal government has quietly stacked the ABC's board with political appointees hostile to the ABC's mission and its claims on public funding. Ministerial interventions into its activities have been frequent and often public, and there has been persistent criticism of the broadcaster's priorities, performance and corporate culture.[15] Fortunately, the various independent reviews instituted over the years have largely declined to fully support the implicit political objective of bringing this annoying organisation to heel. This was especially important in the case of the Mansfield review, which was initiated in the late 1990s by then communications minister Richard Alston with the unstated intention of taking it out of news and current affairs altogether.[16]

Nonetheless, any opportunity for promoting claims of bias in the ABC's coverage of news and current affairs is eagerly exploited by politicians and their supporters in the commercial media, even though everyone knows that such accusations routinely come from both sides of the political spectrum.[17] While, of course, there is no denying that there will be grounds for criticism at particular points in time, and it is important that such criticism is heard, there is little evidence of an institutional political bias that is systemic or ongoing.

The Abbott/Turnbull/Morrison government devoted some effort towards denying that the ABC had been politically targeted or that it had been subject to successive budget cuts.[18] However, their government was more or less on its own in arguing this. In response to a claim by the then communications minister, Paul Fletcher, that the Coalition government had 'provided strong and consistent support to the ABC', a 2022 report by journalism academics Ward, Wake, Ricketson and Mullins spluttered in disbelief that this was a 'breathtakingly misleading statement'. Their research, which goes back through budget allocations from 2014 onwards, concludes that the ABC's budget currently faces an accumulation of losses over the last decade that total $1.2 billion.[19] The Albanese government's restoration of the indexation of the ABC's budget and a modest increase in funding are positive steps, but still far from rectifying the situation.

Ward and his colleagues' general analysis, if not their actual calculations, is broadly supported by other commentary and research. Errington and Van Onselen agree that the ABC has been 'bled with tiny cuts over successive budgets'; research from the Australia Institute has claimed that the ABC has suffered cuts of $526 million over the eight years to 2022; and the resolutely fact-based 'Explainer' from Jennifer Duke in *The Sydney Morning Herald* concluded in 2020 that the ABC has 'good reason to complain its funding has been cut in real terms'.[20]

Historically, there has been a significant difference in how Coalition and Labor governments have managed the broadcaster's funding. The ABC's funding has been increased by Labor governments: under Whitlam by 23 per cent, under Hawke/Keating by 26 per cent and under Rudd/Gillard/Rudd by 3 per cent. In contrast, the ABC's real operational funding has decreased during the terms of Coalitions administrations: under Fraser by 6 per cent, under Howard by 8 per cent and under Abbott/

Turnbull/Morrison by 7 per cent. On Ward and his colleagues' projections, government funding for the ABC in 2025–26 was set to be at its lowest level in real terms in forty-five years. And this comes at a time when the ABC is doing more than ever in the broadcasting, multichannel and digital media environments: it runs six television channels, more than sixty capital-city, local and digital radio stations, four national radio services, an enormous suite of online resources, and live music performances.[21]

There is nothing new, of course, in politicians taking issue with the ABC's coverage of politics. This goes back, at least, to the early 1970s and ABC TV's *This Day Tonight*, when the producers took the cheeky step of having the host interview an empty chair after a politician declined to appear. (Refusing to appear was a common strategy for politicians at the time, designed to prohibit the story from running: without their participation, the program would be unable to demonstrate 'balance'.)[22] What is relatively new is the persistence, the intensity and the categorical character of the contemporary campaign against the ABC.

Rather than being provoked by a particular story or commentary, Coalition governments' denigration of the ABC became constitutive – it is simply how they have talked about it. ('When did you last hear a government minister say anything remotely positive about the ABC?' ask Ricketson and Mullins.[23]) The cuts in funding came in regular strikes against the enemy – each far from critical in itself but wreaking a considerable cumulative effect. One might surmise that their purpose was not only about forcing the ABC to do what it does with much less, putting strain on the organisation and its people, but also about reminding it of the consequences of an adversarial relation with government.[24]

Funding, however, is merely one element within a more programmatic and ideological project, which former prime minister Kevin Rudd has described as an 'unrelenting campaign of bullying, intimidation and delegitimisation'.[25] Indeed, delegitimisation may well be the principal goal, with the objective of stripping the ABC of its standing as a public good. If ever that goes, the case for the ABC to be funded by the taxpayer goes with it (and it is worth remembering that in 2018 the Liberal Party's annual council voted by a two-thirds majority to sell off the ABC). This is how Ricketson and Mullins, in their recent book on the ABC, read the situation. They claim that the Coalition government's purpose was to 'carp and grind away at any and everything, large and small, real or not, to build a picture of the ABC as a hopelessly bloated, biased organisation that despite its name is somehow at root un-Australian'.[26] When the Coalition refused to agree to a leaders' debate hosted by the ABC during the 2022 federal election campaign, journalist and commentator Rick Morton interpreted this as part of a deliberate strategy of 'excising the ABC out of public life'.[27] As it struggles to deal with what has long been a battle for its continued existence, Rudd argues, the national broadcaster has been 'gradually tamed', relinquishing much of the confidence and courage it ideally requires to do its job. It is important to recognise that this is the result of a party political strategy in pursuit of an inherently anti-democratic objective: reining in the power of journalism that serves the public interest.

Underpinning all of this are the culture wars that have been running since at least the election of the Howard government, and which have sought to stall progressive cultural change by using them as a tool to incite social, cultural and political division.[28] The most longstanding battleground for the culture wars has been the campaign against the supposed cultural influence of what political conservatives characterise as latte-sipping, tree-hugging, left-leaning, 'inner-city' or 'cultural' 'elites'. These are among the labels preferred by the culture warriors in the Murdoch press and by their supporters on Sky News After Dark. The most recent versions of the campaign against these 'cultural elites' have accused them of driving 'cancel culture' and the 'woke' interest in progressive issues such as Indigenous rights, climate change, gender equity and sexual identities.

It should go without saying that anxiety about the putative power of this 'inner-city cultural elite' is largely confected. It is risible for such a dominant and powerful organisation as News Corp, for instance, to cast itself as the victim of an entity it more or less constructed itself, and then to claim to have been 'silenced'. However, this characterisation has chimed with conservative resentment at cultural change and fear of the possible social, political and economic consequences of that change. And, it has to be said, given the essentially philosophical basis for so many of these progressive concerns, the regressively anti-intellectual sinew that remains part of the underbelly of Australian egalitarianism provides support for this side of the culture wars.

The ABC sits right in the middle of this, as 'one front in a broader culture war that ranges from the universities to the arts to the social welfare sector'.[29] Grahame Morris, former adviser to Prime Minister Howard, once notoriously described the ABC as 'our enemy talking to our friends'.[30] Such an assessment is not just about the ABC's political reporting but also about its cultural positioning. The consequence for the nation has been the compromised service to the public good which results from continued political harassment and the steady erosion of resources, and which has led to what many perceive as a deterioration in the quality of the ABC's treatment of public issues and its contribution to Australian culture. For Rudd, it is time for the ABC's leaders to 'toughen up and actually show some leadership in defence of their own institution'.[31]

That's a harsh prescription, perhaps, but reflective of progressives' concern about the situation in which the public broadcaster finds itself. Faced with determined political hostility, as well as commercially motivated attacks from other sections of the media, the ABC's maintenance of its status as incontrovertibly a public good for the nation is crucial to its survival. The shrinking of its capacities in the face of this challenge seriously threatens that status.

Commercialising culture

The culture wars have enveloped other institutions as well. They played a part in the dismissal of claims from the arts and cultural sectors for government support during the pandemic, as well as the inroads into their organisations' budgets prior to that. The effects of the exclusion of the arts industries from JobKeeper during the pandemic were only partially ameliorated by the introduction of some small-scale programs that were grudgingly and belatedly introduced in response to public criticism.

In a passionate article published during the 2022 election campaign, writer Alison Croggon described the determined resistance to providing support for these industries as 'targeted vindictiveness'.[32] That vindictiveness was not directed only at these industries' political or cultural positioning – although certainly the arts and performance industries' engagement in the debates around identity politics, the environment and other hot-button issues had placed them in the firing line. Rather, the target for attacks on the arts and cultural institutions and organisations is precisely their status as a public good – their social and cultural significance as something that should be funded in its own right. While there remains a conservative reverence for some of the more traditional, 'elite' artforms such as opera, as well as for the more traditional touchstones of high culture (typically Shakespeare), this does not necessarily extend to a fundamental appreciation of the importance of arts and culture to a sophisticated, open and liberal society. Successive federal governments have been disinclined to fund them as public goods in their own right. This has exposed the arts and cultural industries not only to funding cuts but also to pressure to pursue commercial strategies as their only secure route to survival.

Croggon characterised this as the Morrison government's 'campaign to destroy the arts' but it well predates the Morrison government.[33] A report from the MEAA notes that per capita spending on the cultural sector in Australia is currently at 0.9 per cent, behind the OECD average of 1.2 per cent. Spending on the sector has declined by 18.9 per cent since 2007.[34] This figure suggests that arts organisations have long struggled to secure what they regard as adequate funding from governments of both colours, but the Abbott government's attack on the Australia Council in 2014 took things to a new level, removing $15 million from the Australia Council's discretionary funds to be distributed directly by the minister, George Brandis. The outrage this generated from the arts community gave the government some pause over the following four years, and it resorted instead to slightly more cautious reductions to the culture budget.

The pandemic provided an opportunity to punish the sector by neglect, however, and the government made only the most minimal gestures towards industry assistance – and even then focused largely on the ancillary industries (lighting engineers, set builders and so on) rather than on the creatives themselves. This, notwithstanding the inherent precariousness of careers in the industry and the subsequent vulnerability of its practitioners. Independent arts journalist Elissa Blake reported that in February

2021, 'about 45% of all employees in arts and recreation services were in casual roles without access to basic entitlements including holiday and sick leave and superannuation'. 'Job insecurity', she said, was 'endemic'.[35]

The arts and recreation services were hit harder than any other industry during the pandemic, according to Alison Pennington and Ben Eltham's study for the Centre for Future Work (which drew upon the Australian Bureau of Statistics' *Business Impacts of COVID-19* survey). The survey revealed that 53 per cent of pre–Covid businesses in the sector had ceased operating by April 2020. Pennington and Eltham also point to data gathered by Live Performance Australia, which claims that the performance industries lost $24 billion in potential output, and 79,000 actual jobs over the first year of Covid. In Victoria, a survey of the arts and music industry found that 74 per cent of music workers had experienced a decrease in income; engagement in full-time work had fallen from 34 per cent to 7 per cent of all employed. Most alarming was the finding that 44 per cent of respondents reported losing all of their music-related paid work during the pandemic.[36]

Notwithstanding that level of destruction, and despite criticism of the cruelty of their approach during the pandemic, the Coalition's 2022 federal budget mounted a full-scale attack. The overall cut proposed to the public arts and cultural bodies amounted to 20 per cent.[37] Restart Investment to Sustain and Expand (RISE), the pandemic assistance program for the arts sector, was not renewed, and in any case it had been driven by a decision to support the private profits of commercial companies rather than public institutions, individual artists or smaller arts organisations. Support for regional arts was halved, while funding for Indigenous Arts, the National Gallery of Australia, the National Library of Australia, the National Archives and the National Museum of Australia was cut substantially. This hit institutions already struggling to manage the effects of more than a decade of cuts before the pandemic.

The imposition of 'efficiency dividends' (a budget-reduction strategy that goes back to the Hawke government, but was given a boost under Abbott) had eaten away at the capacity of these institutions, making it difficult even for bodies such as the National Library to do their jobs. Recent news reports have the National Gallery facing a $265 million shortfall in funding, contemplating large-scale staff sackings and even closing its doors for two days each week. Such consequences would have come as no surprise to the Morrison government, of course, and it seems that the howls of pain from the sectors affected did little to shift the government's resolve. Indeed, as Errington and Van Onselen observe, 'to borrow a line often used about Donald Trump, sometimes the cruelty is the point'.[38]

In any reckoning of the national interest, such a strategy is not just politically vindictive but also economically perverse. As Elissa Blake reported at the time, the arts and culture sector employed more than 350,000 people, which is more than three times the number employed in aviation and mining – both industries given privileged funding support by government.[39] The 2020 Insight report from the arts and culture think tank A New Approach claims that Australians employed within the cultural and creative sector amount to 8.1 per cent of the Australian workforce, and generate 6.4 per cent of GDP.[40] No matter, Croggon responds, since 'economic justifications for culture hold no water for governments that are less interested in social good than in ideologically reforming society into their own image'.[41] Admittedly, as the establishment of A New Approach itself recognised, the cultural sector has often suffered from confused public advocacy. This is in part due to the fact that it is both a public service and a cutting-edge industry, an ambiguity which Treasury departments find uncomfortable. As a result, the cultural sector routinely finds itself in two minds about how to proceed when seeking to make a case for support or investment.[42]

Other institutions which suffer from similar confusions of status have been targeted as well. The Coalition's 2022 federal budget levied major cuts to the funding for institutions charged with protecting the public good but which have frustrated governments politically in the past (and, indeed, which they have from time to time attempted to abolish), such as the Human Rights Commission and the National Audit Office.[43] Others caught in this net have been politically benign, but it seems that their function or significance had escaped the attention of those in government. An example is the National Archives, which were bailed out, temporarily and at the last minute, in 2021 when that attention deficit was addressed through a public campaign from the nation's historians.

The lack of interest in funding institutions dedicated to the public good has motivated governments to seize on strategies of commercialisation as a means of making the problem go away. This is especially the case for the culture and heritage sectors.[44] As noted earlier, the Keating government's *Creative Nation* blueprint for cultural policy, released in 1994, broadly accepted that support for the production of culture was an appropriate and necessary activity for government. However, by the time we reach its successor in 2013, the Gillard government's *Creative Australia*, it had become almost routine for cultural policy to be framed around the notion that cultural activities should be able to demonstrate their value in the marketplace. They should seek commercial viability rather than rely on continued government subvention.[45] As Tony Bennett and his co-editors note in the introduction to their landmark sociological study of cultural consumption in

Australia, successive governments have since reversed most of the directions taken in *Creative Nation*. In particular, 'the levels of funding for, and autonomy of, funding bodies like the Australia Council were reduced', while 'market principles were championed against the values of public-ness in both the cultural sector … and the education system'.[46]

Indeed, I would argue that the largest-scale and most deleterious commercialising strategy targeting public institutions has been in relation to the university sector.

Capping the 'wellspring of ideas'

When the pandemic hit and the Morrison government set out its survival package for workers and employers across the economy, the public universities were deliberately excluded. With campuses closed, enrolments effectively put on pause and international students gone, university revenues were drastically affected. However, the eligibility criteria for JobKeeper were designed in such a way that universities could not qualify, while JobSeeker was also denied to international students – even though this might have been a way of keeping them in the system (and in the country). As George Megalogenis has pointed out, 'Given the gargantuan sums being borrowed and spent on the safety net, no one needed to be worse off.'[47]

The impact on staff and students was dramatic. Estimates vary as to the number of jobs lost (due to the way the universities classify their full-time staff), but Megalogenis's figure of 30,000, or just under 12 per cent of the sector, sits in the middle of the pack (the range of the estimates is from 20,000 to 40,000 jobs lost).[48] One of Australia's most eminent analysts of higher education policy, Professor Frank Larkins, has pointed out that 65 per cent of these job losses were those of casual staff, despite them only making up 14 per cent of employed staff nationally.[49]

Casual staff at universities are mostly young and at the beginning of their careers. Typically, they are recent graduates from postgraduate programs, who patch together whatever sessional teaching hours they can, often across multiple campuses and usually for years, while they try to secure their first permanent appointment. These people are both the bedrock and the future of the sector. In some institutions, anecdotal evidence indicates, they have been used to perform anything up to 80 per cent of universities' undergraduate teaching, and they have been the object of considerable national investment in their education and training. Now, at least 20,000 of them are gone – probably never to return. (And we are speaking of 'full-time equivalent' positions, so the actual number of individuals leaving the system will be much higher.)

The pandemic's border restrictions cut off the supply of international students overnight. Successive federal governments had pushed the university sector to commercialise over the previous two decades, so they had expanded their sources of non-government income by increasing their intake of international students. They did this very successfully – to the point that, in some of the 'sandstone' universities, international students might comprise up to a third of total enrolments.[50] But then, as economics editor for *The Sydney Morning Herald* Ross Gittins noted, after the universities had managed to generate so much of their funding from overseas students, and when the coronavirus obliged the government to ban foreign travellers, it hung the universities 'out to dry'. To add insult to injury, the universities were then criticised because 'they should never have allowed themselves to become so dependent on a single source of revenue'.[51]

Far from regretting the harshness of their treatment of the sector in 2020 and 2021, the Coalition's March 2022 budget further cut the share of the 2023 education budget going to higher education to a record low of 23.5 per cent. By way of comparison, federal funding for non-government schools in that year was projected to be at an all-time high of 35.7 per cent of the national education budget. Spending on higher education was then budgeted to fall even further in absolute terms over the next two years. By 2023–24, Megalogenis reported, 'spending will be 10.3 per cent lower than when the sector was being short-changed during the pandemic itself'.[52] There has been some slight amelioration of this outlook, with the allocation of 20,000 new (but targeted) places for higher education in the October 2022 federal budget, but many of the more concerning elements of higher education funding instituted under the Coalition have so far remained in place.

As Judith Brett has commented in response to this treatment of what she describes as 'traditionally the wellspring of ideas', 'surely it cannot be in the national interest to weaken Australian universities' capacities to teach and do research'.[53] Surely not, but that is exactly what has happened. When Megalogenis tried to find out why the Coalition had taken such a brutal approach, and why universities had been so clearly singled out, the answer he got from 'one person familiar with the government's thinking' was: 'It's not that complicated. The government hates universities.'[54] That's it. The full justification offered for the Coalition's treatment of the Australian public university system is that the government 'hates' universities! It is actually quite staggering to realise that, in order to indulge such a prejudice, and in complete disregard of the government's responsibility to protect even the most basic conception of the national interest, the universities were treated as if they were expendable.[55]

Like so many other flaws in our national polity that the pandemic has exposed, what has become a toxic relation between government and the university sector didn't start then (I would trace its beginnings back to the imposition of the Unified National System during the Hawke/Keating government), but it certainly ramped up over the term of the Abbott/Turnbull/Morrison governments. It went from difficult but manageable to the point where the government's hostility stood in the way of any kind of sensible higher education policy development.[56]

As the political purchase of the idea of the public good diminishes, universities present a problem for populist governments in market democracies. Stefan Collini has pointed out that there are only two forms of justification that such governments assume will be accepted by their electorates. The first refers to the role of universities in training and skills development for the nation's workforce, while the second is focused on certain benefits of research – mostly medical, technological or economic benefits. There are other ways of defining the value of universities, of course, such as their fundamental role in the production and dissemination of knowledge, in creating a well-educated population, or in the preservation, cultivation and transmission of cultural traditions and civic values.[57] But, in a context so comprehensively distorted by the divisions created by the culture wars in Australia, these are all politically unpalatable.

The Coalition's 'older, whiter electoral base sees the universities as enemy ground, representing Labor's younger, cosmopolitan base', Megalogenis points out.[58] This results in the prioritisation of the most instrumentalist justification for universities, exemplified by the ham-fisted attempts at 'vocationalisation' that lay behind the 'Job-ready Graduates Package'.[59] (The Job-ready Graduates Package, introduced in 2022, increased the cost of a humanities degree by 113 per cent, a decision justified by the incorrect claim that humanities graduates find it harder to get jobs than science graduates.)

The present policy approaches – so far including those of the current Labor government – suggest that our federal governments have effectively reduced the function of higher education to delivering a private good to individuals. Gone is any recognition of the broader public good that comes from what remains of the more fundamental intellectual, educational, civic, social and cultural purposes of the university.

It must be acknowledged, regrettably, that the universities haven't been particularly brave in standing up for these fundamental purposes. Trapped by a continual game of bait-and-switch, they have attempted to appease a hostile government by agreeing to one egregious proposal so that they might do better with the next. The time has long gone for university vice-chancellors to strenuously mount more than an economistic or vocational defence for their institutions' continued existence. They have effectively acceded to the idea that universities should think of themselves as businesses (they aren't, and therefore they shouldn't) and that they should marketise their operations to meet the demands of their 'customers' (this they have done, at scale, and look where it has taken them). Over time, this has substantially eroded what was previously a uniquely collegial practice of university administration, and the trust between university staff and university management.

For many in the sector now, university managers seem to be pursuing an entirely different model of the university to the one their employees signed up for. There are many indicators of this. The massive increase in casual appointments across the sector, and the longstanding trick of cross-subsidising research investment by raiding the budget for teaching, may have served the corporate interests of the university but they have not served those of staff or students, or improved the quality and sustainability of the system. Most egregiously, it appears that certain universities that cut their expenses by sacking large numbers of staff during Covid under the cover of budget emergency ended up returning substantial operating surpluses at the end of 2021. This may have improved their standing as businesses, but over time will be condemned as a failure of their responsibility to maintain the quality of their institutions, their commitment to their staff, the human capacity of the sector as a whole and their contribution to the public good.

While rank-and-file academic staff have long protested their situation, they are routinely written off by government, the media and even their own administrators as privileged and self-interested whingers, so it has largely been left to others to make the contrary argument to the public.[60] As newspaper columnist Elizabeth Farrelly writes in her caustic assessment of the marketisation of the university, seeing education as being 'about individual career trajectories is reductivist nonsense. Educating the educable, especially in the history of ideas, is about the culture we make. It is our best defence against world collapse. Education is survival.'[61]

Seeking support by emphasising the economic importance of the sector (it is our third-largest export industry) has not only been unsuccessful, but it is also, I would contend, the wrong strategy. Stefan Collini has commented (in the UK context) that those defending the universities there have too often fallen into the trap of choosing to justify higher education as an activity we continue to fund 'because it yields incidental benefits which are popular with those not in a position to appreciate the activity's intrinsic interest and worth'.[62]

In the meantime, we find ourselves stuck with a damaged university sector in which federal funding, staffing levels, curricula and course offerings (and next, inevitably, international reputations) have all shrunk dramatically, while the cost of many degrees and the numbers of domestic students have all increased. Better funding arrangements are certainly an imperative, but that can only be a first step towards repairing what is now a broken system.

In their history of the Australian university sector, *No End of a Lesson*, Stuart Macintyre, André Brett and Gwilym Croucher examine the changes to higher education instituted under Labor by education minister John Dawkins in 1987. These shaped the environment for higher education from that time on. Among other things, the 'Dawkins revolution' made the institutions directly accountable to government, forced them to think of themselves as businesses and tied the support of research more closely to what the government considered to be the nation's economic interests. Dawkins' Unified National System generated an expansion in enrolments that was, paradoxically, paired with a serious trimming of university budgets. Between 1996 and 2001, the numbers of students increased from 581,000 to 614,000 but Commonwealth funding fell from $5108 million to $4588 million. The funding for each HECS student fell from $12,104 to $9892. This amounted to a cut of 18 per cent over the five years. Universities were forced to make up the shortfall in government funding with an increase in student fees and, as noted earlier, by expanding their international student intake.[63]

When I was starting my career as a university teacher in the 1970s, the federal government was contributing up to 90 per cent of university budgets; by 2001 that share had fallen to 46 per cent. This had an effect. By the time of the Bradley Review of Australian Higher Education, which was commissioned in 2007 and reported in 2008, Australians were being told that our system was 'falling behind other countries in participation and quality, overly reliant on international fee income and in urgent need of additional investment'.[64] Little was done to fix this, and it has only got worse in the years since.

If we fast-forward to the contemporary situation, and while there is debate over how this kind of funding gets measured, the Australian Bureau of Statistics tells us that the allocation to higher education from all levels of government between 2017 and 2021 declined by over 39 per cent. It isn't likely to get much better. The current projections of university funding in 2023–24 put it at $9.3 billion, which may sound a lot but is actually, in real terms, more or less the same as it was in 2009–10, when the system was far smaller and the costs much lower.[65]

Those who have analysed the university sector have all sung their concerns from very much the same songsheet, and over a very long period.[66] It is hard to imagine any informed observer looking at the current state of the Australian university sector without expressing alarm. At the time of writing, Public Universities Australia, a newly formed grassroots collaborative group representing much of the sector, is calling for a 'summit' to discuss how to address the crisis in our universities.[67] The present education minister, Jason Clare, has also instituted a consultative review of the sector, the Universities Accord, that at least recognises there are some important issues to be investigated. Without the political will to introduce substantial change, however, the same problems will remain, the same settings will produce the same results, and the same forces will be to blame.

Why is it so?

American professor of public policy Robert Reich has presented a searing critique of how the workings of the 'free market' have delivered extraordinary power to 'moneyed interests' and 'economic elites' in the United States, to the detriment of the common good. Those interests, he says, have failed to use that power to deliver 'rising or even stable incomes and jobs to most of the rest of the nation'. As their concern for the common good has dwindled, Reich says, they have focused ever more intently on 'rig[ging] the system for their own benefit'. He emphasises the scale of the opportunity that has been lost as these sectors gained in wealth and power, but chose to use these gains only to consolidate their own position and privilege. They could, he says, have 'made a different choice':

> They could have used their political and economic clout to get better schools for all, comprehensive job retraining, wage insurance, better public transportation, and expanded unemployment insurance. They could have pushed for universal health insurance. They could have paid for all this by accepting, even lobbying for, higher taxes on themselves. They could have strengthened rather than fought off unions, and pushed for laws giving workers more rather than less voice. They could have demanded limits on campaign spending.[68]

Instead, 'they did the reverse: they spent more and more of their ever-expanding wealth to alter the rules of the game to their own advantage.' And, Reich concludes, 'we are now living with the consequences'.

There is a striking parallel in Australia.[69] As the public good recedes further from view, and as the institutions most dedicated to its service find themselves reeling from political attacks and the consequences of targeted underfunding, one has to ask why this has occurred here. Why, indeed, have we *allowed* it to occur here?

Providing a simple explanation for this is not easy. There are so many contending influences on the diminution of the public good and the attack on our institutions, and they are all subject to political debate. Just as Reich has noted in relation to the United

States, in Australia we have suffered from the neoliberal preference for the market as the best mechanism for the distribution of opportunity, with the acquisition of wealth positioned as the core objective for business and for individuals. Hollywood, with its ear ever tuned to the zeitgeist, summed it up through Gordon Gekko's mantra in the 1987 film *Wall Street*: 'greed is good'.

Also implicated here is the sidelining of programs of 'nationing' that could have better protected or even advanced the public values that endow these institutions with their significance and underpin their social and cultural centrality. Instead, it would appear, a weakening in the community's understanding of the public good has allowed some of our democratic state's basic furniture – such as a public broadcaster – to be opportunistically framed as a luxury or an indulgence. Governments in Australia have seized upon commercialisation as a handy strategy for outsourcing the difficulty of making political choices about funding and investment priorities. This has enabled the offloading of tricky problems about what to do with non-profit but institutionally established government authorities and agencies.

Most importantly, there is something which is actually quite specific to the fate of the institutions we have examined in this chapter. That is the desire within successive federal governments, prosecuted in collaboration with sections of the media, to discredit any challenges to their authority, competence and public credibility that might come from independent and trusted sources of knowledge, expertise and ideas. In relation to the university sector, this desire has a long history. Both major parties, Professor Stephen Knight suggests, 'bitterly resented the criticism they suffered from campus figures, staff and students alike, through the 1970s, and this hostility evidently meshed with the largely right-wing media dislike of academics as both independent and respected'.[70]

Finally, there is the shrinkage of the purpose of politics in recent years, as it has become single-mindedly focused on securing power rather than on governing in the national interest. Underlying all of these considerations, and one of the most difficult issues for Australians to address in the future, is the decline in the understanding of, the responsibility to and the generation of a sense of belonging and community within the nation.

CHAPTER 6

What's to be done?

'Communities are distinguished, not by their falsity/genuineness, but by the style in which they are imagined.'

Benedict Anderson[1]

Given the considerable obstacles to the construction of a common culture canvassed so far in this book, just how are Australians to go about building points of consensus and a focus for a shared imagination of what the nation might be? Will our recent history of social fragmentation and political division bar us from making anything like a decent fist of such a project? And, too, is there any longer so much at stake in the project of nation formation as was once the case?

The contemporary role of the nation-state has undergone a significant shift in purpose and meaning. Since the 1990s, the project of nation formation has gradually moved into the background in most Western democracies, as they have directed their attention outwards, searching for a trading profile within the competitive markets of a globalising economy. For some, that search led to an investment in what came to be called 'nation-branding'.[2] This label refers to the promotion – and, in some cases, the frank invention – of commercially framed national identities in order to address global markets rather than the national community. (Think Tony Blair's 'Cool Britannia', or, across the Tasman, '100% New Zealand'.) Typically, the development and marketing of these identities took place at some distance from the nation's citizenry, their location and in some cases even from their histories.[3]

Covid-19 changed much of that. Early on, many believed the expansion of the global economy would reduce the relevance and power of the nation-state even as it increased the utility of the national brand. However, this proposition was always contested, and had already begun to fracture before the arrival of Covid-19 sent it into reverse.[4] Global trade flows stopped at national borders, the movement of people did so as well, and nations such as Australia suddenly had to confront the short-sightedness which lay behind the sacrifice of their sovereign capacity for the onshore manufacturing of essential items for domestic consumption. Countries which had built their neoliberal dream on globalisation, small government, market forces and the privatisation of public utilities suddenly had to consider the 'return of the state'.[5] In the end, it was the national capacity for managing the health and social welfare of its citizens which most came under the spotlight. In Australia, as we have seen, that spotlight revealed the consequences of decades of privatisation, underfunding and neglect.

While I maintain that there is certainly a point to the continuing project of nation formation, it is also important to acknowledge how radically that project has been transformed. For many years, political scientist Benedict Anderson's 1983 work *Imagined Communities* was the default reference for our understanding of the construction of the national community, but much of his account has been superseded as social, technological and cultural changes have unfolded.[6]

Earlier, it was understood that the formation and maintenance of national communities came from citizens' participation in shared experiences. These ranged from public rituals and celebrations of belonging (such as official memorial events or attendance at major sporting events) to everyday routines of domestic consumption (such as reading the daily newspaper). Traditionally, the mass media played a central role in such processes. People took their news, information and entertainment from a limited number of sources, and they participated in national, regional and local conversations that drew upon those sources. At the level of everyday life, people watched many of the same shows on television at the same times, and listened to radio programs that spoke to and about their local and regional communities. They took those experiences with them from the home into the workplace.

In his initial analysis, Anderson foregrounded the role of the print media as the mechanism which influentially bound the community's imaginings of belonging into those of a nation. Even as other mass media, such as broadcast television, complemented and eventually supplanted the newspaper in this regard, Anderson's model retained its relevance through its emphasis on the central role of the mass media in constructing the national community.

Over the last twenty years, however, the media has been reinvented, and Anderson's conception no longer so readily fits the circumstances. Not only has the press lost much of its cultural and political dominance, but the mass media in general, including television, have done so as well.

Furthermore, as Andreas Hepp has shown, the nature of the media's influence on society and culture has fundamentally changed. Since it is no longer addressing us as a mass audience, the media's influence is now more dispersed, more differentiated, more individualised, less centralised, but also even more pervasive. Hepp describes what he calls the 'mediatization' of everyday life, a process through which our use of media (broadly defined to include personal computers and mobile devices such as phones and tablets) now 'moulds' our social existence.[7] This 'moulding' is accomplished through multiple points of insertion into the routines and practices of our everyday lives. So, this is not just when we are watching television or reading a newspaper, but it also shapes how we shop, how and where we access the news, and how we connect with friends, workmates and family – some of the things we talked about briefly in the discussion of automation in Chapter 4.

Of course, the various forms of social media play a significant part in this, and they have consequently become an important location for examining, on the one hand, the construction of the 'community' that they enable and, on the other hand, their implication in the patterns of social fragmentation and political polarisation discussed earlier in this book. This alerts us to the importance of digital media as new modes of intervention into the construction of our culture and society. Under their influence, and again as suggested earlier, we are experiencing a major reconfiguration of the social.

Disaster zones: The community and the state

The idea of the imagined community as a means of describing the experience of belonging to a nation depends upon a sense of 'co-presence'. This is the imagined connection between the individual citizen and the millions of other individuals – whom they do not know and will never meet – who with them make up the population of the nation. This shared sense of the national community, some have argued, has diminished in recent years. Let's consider what that looks like.

The ABC TV drama *Fires*, first screened in 2021, is a miniseries based upon events that occurred during the Black Summer bushfires of 2019–20. Its six episodes follow a group of characters and their communities as they confront the most catastrophic fire season Australia has experienced. Powerful and moving, it does an extraordinary job of bringing the experiences of these communities vividly to the screen. Some of the stories are familiar to us – not exact re-creations, but lightly fictionalised versions of incidents we might recognise from the news reports at the time. Episode Five explores the terrible choices those fighting the fires must make, balancing the needs of so many endangered people against their limited capacity to help everyone who requires it.

One of the lead characters in this episode, Ruth, a proud and fiercely independent woman whose house has been lost to the fire, is confronted with her small town's destruction and the death of one of the young volunteer firefighters. When the media turn up to interview the citizens of her township of Curran, a TV reporter asks the assembled group if they are aware of public criticism of 'Australia's response to the fires'. Ruth, aggrieved and angry, comes forward, addressing precisely that imagined co-presence of the nation in order to focus its attention not only upon the town's devastation but also upon the community's sense of abandonment. 'Young people are dying,' she protests, 'before they even have a life.' As the camera moves into close-up, her fury spills out: 'How bad does it have to get,' she yells, 'before someone actually does something? Isn't *this* enough? *Isn't it?*'

This resonates: Australians know about this. They know how communities were destroyed, how the volunteers of the fire and rescue services and those running the State Emergency Services (SES) were overwhelmed as several fire fronts converged into a 'megafire', and how the federal government dragged its feet, disgracefully, in responding. All of this is condensed in the popular mind in the image of the prime minister on holiday in Hawaii instead of leading the national response. As a demonstration of the disconnection between the community and the state, this couldn't have been clearer.

But it got worse. While communities were uniting in solidarity to protect themselves and their neighbours, at times risking their lives, the federal government chose to politicise the disaster. It deflected criticism of its response by mounting an attack on those pointing to the influence of climate change upon the scale and spread of the fires. Dismissing those experts who might have provided informed advice, the federal government's primary objective was to ensure that no blame for these events, or the way they were handled, should be attached to it.

Eventually, a program of relief and recovery was developed, but the history of neglect did not stop there. Years down the track, many of these people and their communities are yet to receive the support they were promised.[8] Communities were left to forge a way ahead by themselves (as another ABC TV series, *People's Republic of Mallacoota*, documents). In *Fires* and in the events it depicts, the community and the national government no longer productively intersect. Trust in the nation and its interest in its citizens' wellbeing is undermined. These are events in which the idea of the shrinking nation is, compellingly, given substance.

More or less the same scenario repeated itself during the Northern Rivers floods in New South Wales in early 2022. Once again, the community rose to the occasion, showing a determination and resilience that could only be admired. As lives were placed at risk by the rising floodwaters, SES services were thin on the ground. At the time, it was reported, the flood-prone town of Lismore (with a population of 40,000) had only two boats for the SES to use. It was left to the local residents, in their tinnies and kayaks and dinghies and jetskis, to trawl the rising waters, rescuing homeowners who had been stranded, sometimes for hours, on their roofs in the rain waiting for assistance. (One woman was delighted to find that the person driving the jetski that rescued her was the champion surfer Mick Fanning.[9]) It was almost a week before there was any significant state presence on the ground, and even longer before the army was called in to help with the clean-up and recovery. At least the New South Wales premier, Dominic Perrottet, had the courage to front the public while he toured the devastation of Lismore, but Prime Minister Morrison was so leery of his likely reception that he was helicoptered in to deal only with the town's officials.

At the time of this writing, more than one year on, many hundreds of locals are still waiting for assistance, almost a thousand remain homeless, and while there are now the beginnings of an action plan for recovery and reconstruction, Lismore is still very much a disaster zone.[10]

The anger Ruth expresses in her outburst at the end of *Fires*, channelling the real frustration we have seen expressed in news reports by members of communities in places such as Cobargo, Merimbula and Coraki, is a response to the nation's failure to protect and care for its citizens. This is a 'we should be better than this' moment, as the 'someone' Ruth addresses is the successive national governments who have cynically and irresponsibly allowed this situation to develop: first by doggedly prosecuting the climate wars for political advantage, and then by procrastinating and blame-shifting rather than immediately responding to citizens' cries for help.

The positive message to come out of this is the strength of the communities, the power of local connections to each other and to their place. The negative is what has gone missing – the sense of belonging that connects local communities to the nation-state. The events that occurred in these disaster zones call up the importance of that sense of belonging; it is evident in the sense of outrage and abandonment experienced by communities forced to deal with the state's failure to live up to its responsibilities to its citizens. If this is in fact a 'we should be better than this' moment, then the way to fix it is for Australia to get better at being a nation.

The media, the digital and the national community

'Being a nation', let alone 'getting better' at it, however, has become harder than it used to be. The means to such an end are no longer quite as self-evident as they might once have been. When the mass media were the only game in town, they provided something like a baseline platform for the construction of a common national culture. They routinely, albeit in various ways, reflected a common set of values, a working agreement on issues of fact, and an orientation towards an assessment of the national interest that was, again, varied, but that largely remained within broadly accepted ethical and political guardrails.

If we go back to, say, the early 1980s, Australia was hardwired into a national community by the combination of three national commercial television networks, two nationally networked public broadcasters and several national commercial radio networks. That was all there was. Also, and this is perhaps hard to remember now, this was a time when the news was still dominated by factual reporting rather than opinion, and the limited competition between media outlets meant there was less incentive for turning information into entertainment as a means of winning the battle for declining audiences. Over the three decades since its introduction, television had become particularly important to the building of a national community through its unique capacity to gather the collective attention of the national audience. It had also become extensively embedded into the routines of daily life, and what Daniel Dayan calls its 'sharedness' meant that it was continually feeding into conversations and interactions between people inside and outside the home that were, in a sense, everyday performances of belonging and community.[11]

Of course, the political downside to the dominance of a highly concentrated mass media at that time was the limited diversity and the significant patterns of exclusion that underpinned the media's selection of their sources of information and the people from whom they sought an opinion. However, while the 1990s' reinvention of the media offered the possibility of greater diversity and inclusiveness as competition to the traditional mass media expanded, it also brought the possibility of an outcome that we are now experiencing: that it would impact 'on television's influence on the structure and practice of everyday life, and perhaps eventually also upon the cogency of a sense of national community', as Anna Cristina Pertierra and I wrote in 2013.[12]

As that timeline suggests, there were infrastructural and technological changes driving what would eventually bring a much greater degree of contingency to the relation between the media and the national community. Obviously, there are fundamental differences between the media environment I am invoking as belonging to that previous era and what we are experiencing now, and these differences have produced new forms of social connection. The multichannel environment for television, which arrived with the introduction of pay TV in the early 1990s, slices its audiences up into individual taste fractions rather than encouraging them to share the experience of watching what everybody else is watching. The social networks enabled by the multichannel and online environment – 'virtual, transnational, vernacular, customized to the consumer's preferences', as Pertierra and I noted – have turned out to be very different to those which had preceded them, which were 'national, geo-politically located, institutionalized and centralized'. Most significantly, these new communities have tended to locate themselves in a media space – within Facebook, for instance – rather than in a national space.[13]

The increase in competition across platforms also affected how the mass media behaved. As time went on, it was no longer so easy to argue that they served as a baseline for the values of a common culture. As I observed earlier, commercial television news and current affairs relinquished much of its interest in serving the public good and focused instead on whatever it took to attract what the industry likes to call 'eyeballs'. This meant that the more socially nourishing elements of political and social analysis largely disappeared from commercial television current-affairs programming, and were replaced by a fast-food diet of bad neighbours, consumer scams, 'love rat' exposures, dole-bludger beat-ups, and 'health stories' promoting the latest fads for dealing with chronic back pain, cosmetic surgery, weight loss or cellulite.

Radio, for its part, came up with the figure of the shock-jock. They depended on getting their listeners sufficiently engaged to phone in, and they did this by generating resentment, fear and anger in any way they could. The emergence of commercial radio 'talkback' hosts such as Stan Zemanek and Alan Jones took the level of disinformation, prejudice and malice on Australian radio to a new level.[14] The Strike Force Neil report found that some of Sydney's talkback radio hosts had played a part in fomenting the race hatred that culminated in the Cronulla race riots in 2005.[15]

As for the daily print media, they chose to address a more segmented audience than previously. Those sections of the print media most closely aligned with News Corp's corporate agendas (that is, almost 70 per cent of the sector) increasingly hitched their reporting of the news to partisan political campaigns. In order to do this, the distinction between fact and opinion was gradually wound back. Opinion pages right across the print media became more thoroughly politicised. The analyses from the two main proprietors – Nine Media (formerly Fairfax) and News Corp – often read as if they are coming from two different planets.

The sum effect of all these shifts, regrettably, has been to turn much of the mass media into mechanisms of division – for the splintering of the national community, not for its construction or confirmation.

The impact of such tendencies has been substantial. The multichannel environment for broadcast television, further expanded by the arrival of the transnational streaming services, has seriously limited the capacity for television to play a significant daily role in the construction of a national culture. The transnational framework of so much of the dominant social media platforms has loosened their participants' connection to their geopolitical location. The individualisation of online newsfeeds and recommendations concentrates upon the fashioning of the personal identities of individual participants more than upon the interests of the community. Talk radio has capitalised upon an implicit but ongoing relaxation of community standards in what it is allowed to say, and consistently crosses the line separating what might be regarded as the legitimate expression of opinion from the irresponsible incitement of division, anger and hatred. And as they struggle to maintain their readership and their relevance, most of our print media have settled for targeting particular interest groups for their messaging, even while pretending to speak to the nation as a whole.

From the point of view of those seeking to maintain a functional and inclusive national community, this might be regarded as a pretty depressing landscape. Nevertheless, and despite all that, Australians have still managed to find ways to share mass-mediated and collective national experiences. Most often, however, they tend to be event-based – big national sporting events, for instance, or moments of celebration or memorial – rather than quotidian. They still mostly occur via television, and so the status of the 'national broadcaster' has continued to be a coveted asset, particularly for the commercial networks.

Both the Nine and Seven networks have pitched their claims to be the 'national network' at various points over the last decade or so – such as when hosting leaders' debates for federal elections or covering the funeral of Queen Elizabeth II in 2022. However, when there are moments of emergency or national crisis, the reach of the ABC's national broadcasting network reasserts itself. It is the only service that is universally available via both television and radio, and it has long been the most trusted. Not only is it comparatively free from commercial considerations in deciding on its content, but it can also – because it does not have to deal with advertisers – decide unilaterally to vary its schedule when circumstances demand. In recent years, with fires, floods and the pandemic propelling all parts of the nation from one major crisis to another, that capacity has been fully deployed and publicly appreciated. It is perhaps in the active engagement of the ABC at such moments of national need that we see the best of our efforts to continue to work together as a nation, and a compelling reason why we might want to continue to do so.

The idea of the nation, however, can work in politically contradictory ways. On the one hand, the nation can offer the security of belonging to those who wish to identify with it, but on the other hand the nation can also be exclusivist if it becomes selective in who it will allow to belong. Scott Morrison, notoriously, told us that those who 'have a go' would 'get a go' – a formulation that explicitly qualifies any expectations of the certainty of belonging.

As an idea, nationalism is in many ways an empty vessel, and it is politics more than geography which determines how that vessel gets filled – how nationalism expresses itself and in whose interests, and how it is put to work to define the character of the nation. The dual potential of nationalism, and the possible downsides of the ways in which the nation defines itself and through which categories, has long raised concerns among those who recognise the dangers residing in this potential. Australia's treatment of Indigenous people, of successive waves of immigrants, of 'queue-jumping' refugees, of the unemployed and disadvantaged, and most recently of the transgender community has revealed just how contingent and strategic inclusion in the nation can be, and how easily categories of exclusion can be invented, installed and publicly rationalised.

Consequently, it is not surprising that alternative modes of belonging and forms of identity have been seen as holding some promise as a means of dislodging the centrality of the nation, and of nationalism, from our construction of our society. Advocates for the growing importance of online social networks have promoted their capacity to build new kinds of communities. Crucially, these new kinds of community are not necessarily determined by where you live, and so have ushered in new possibilities for connection and belonging. As television relinquishes much of its power to construct the national community, the networked online community has become an important component in the more optimistic readings of the political potential of the new media landscape. Welcomed initially as the desired product of pro-social technologies, these networked communities were regarded as 'preferred alternatives to top-down, institutionally driven communities such as those of the state or the nation', as Pertierra and I have written.[16]

More substantially, social networks have proved able to fill significant gaps in social connection that have created long-term patterns of communication disadvantage for particular groups. For some of those in remote or rural locations, for instance, participation in social networks has dramatically enhanced their sense of community and belonging. Indigenous and diasporic communities appear to have been particular beneficiaries of the connections that social networks enable.[17]

However, the wholesale attribution of the term 'community' to describe the character of the online social network does stretch the meaning of the word. Most online 'communities' are de facto personal networks, focused on the construction and maintenance of the participant's personal identity, or they are fan or subscriber sites organised around individualised patterns of media consumption or special interests.[18]

Most significantly, in contrast to how we connect to our (non-virtual) local community, and though they may figure prominently in people's lives, these are not 'communities' where people actually live. In such a social network, there is no equivalent to the extensive patterns of the community-driven rights, obligations and responsibilities that structure the real-world community in which we pursue our everyday lives. Typically, in such a community, there are expectations of behaviour that are explicitly aimed at serving the common good rather than personal interest. It has become very clear that there can be quite a stark difference between the standards of behaviour tolerated online and what would be tolerated in face-to-face interactions offline. Even where there are established protocols of online behaviour which participants are expected to collectively observe, these usually stop well short of 'the extensive patterns of obligation' that structure the practices of everyday life within the community.[19] As a result, as Pertierra and I have argued, while there is certainly strong evidence that social media are highly effective at building personal networks, it is not yet clear that they can offer new ways of building our local communities, or our national ones.[20]

Indeed, some social networks seem to have the opposite intention in mind. Mark Andrejevic cites American social commentator Sherry Turkle's notable recanting of her initial enthusiasm for digital media, where she comes to describe social media as 'fundamentally anti-social technologies'.[21] Turkle was specifically objecting to the commodification of social relations, but that is only one of the concerns that have been raised about the consequences of social media. Social media are now likely to be regarded as a threat to democracy rather than its handmaiden when they are used to propagate extremist politics and spread dangerous disinformation.[22] While they clearly do still serve the pro-social function of giving voice to the many individuals and communities who have found themselves otherwise excluded from mainstream conversations, the degree to which some of those voices have been used for hate speech, bullying, misogynistic and racialist trolling, and extremist political propaganda is alarming. Although the more traditional channels through which the nation talked to and about itself are in decline, exposing a gap in the ways in which the imagined community can be addressed and activated, social media are highly compromised as a means of filling this gap.

Accordingly, it is difficult to imagine how and where the construction of the national community might take place in the future. Indeed, it is possible that the collective experience of the nation is becoming exceptional, with the occasional moment of solidarity or celebration standing out because it is so rare. Judith Brett has suggested that the recent experience of the pandemic, in which there was such a marked difference between the measures taken by the various states and territories and the varied rhetoric from the federal government, might reflect the possibility that Australians were becoming more strongly identified with their state than with their country.[23] The experiences of the last few years have also demonstrated how strongly Australians have identified with their local community.

This is not new, of course. The research project referred to earlier, led by Tony Bennett and examining shifts in Australians' cultural consumption since Keating's *Creative Nation*, conducted a group of interviews with ordinary people about their patterns of cultural participation and belonging over 2016–2018. The comments made in these interviews underlined the continuing importance of the local, as the 'experiences reported demonstrate[d] the continuing relevance of structures of community such as the family, the church, or the local sports club'.[24] The way ahead for a reimagined nation may well need to start at such locations, building the national community from the ground up, from the cultures created at the level of the local or the regional community.

I was reminded of this possibility while reading journalist Damien Cave's recent personal memoir of his adaptation to Australian everyday culture after arriving from America with his wife and children. Among his observations about how differently Australians dealt with the pandemic, by comparison with his compatriots back home, he made an interesting point about the fundamental building blocks to a national sensibility, to that elusive civic disposition that could be found in the local community. 'Australia would never have done as well with the pandemic', Cave wrote, '… if it hadn't first built and supported community clubs and volunteer organisations, for lifesaving, for firefighting, for swimming, while also pushing children to confront their fears in the bush, in the water and in the classroom.'[25]

Perhaps, as we customarily connect the construction of the nation to the bigger, more expansive initiatives driven by state and federal governments, we may be in danger of missing out on the implications of this orientation. The nation may be understood best, actually, as an aggregation of local and regional communities. What they share socially and culturally allows them to amount to something that is more than just the sum of their component parts.

It is worth thinking about this. As the author of *Media Nations*, Sabina Mihelj, claims, 'being a member of a nation' remains 'an indispensable attribute of humanity' in today's world. In 'often hardly noticeable ways', she says, 'national belonging continues to inform people's perceptions of the world, collective memories and expressions of belonging'.[26] Political and social theorist Craig Calhoun defended nations and nationalism at a time when theories of globalisation and cosmopolitanism had forced them onto the back foot, noting nationalism's value as 'a form of social solidarity and one of the background conditions upon which modern democracy has been based'. Even as he recognised the need to direct critical attention to nationalism's 'limits, illusions and potential for abuse', we should not, he warned, 'dismiss it'.[27]

The times have changed now in ways that make these ideas even more cogent than they were when first promulgated. The 'wicked' problems societies face today were once framed as overwhelmingly global rather than national in nature – climate change is the most obvious example – and the capacity for the individual nation-state to influence their resolution was thus thought to be very limited. However, so many of the issues this book has examined, while often dramatically subject to external influences to be sure, nonetheless demand responses that must come from within the nation-state. Accordingly, Australia needs to find ways to make the nation-state more responsive to its citizenry and more productively focused upon serious issues of policy, rather than upon the narcissistic game of party politics.

Those issues must include serious thinking about the construction of community, and about how Australia should go about renewing its interest in supporting the development of a diverse, inclusive and equitable national culture.

The culture wars and their legacy

One major fly in the ointment here is Australia's long history of culture wars. Within that history, the idea of culture has been vigorously deployed as a weapon of division, obstructing precisely the kinds of community-building projects described above. These wars have now spanned decades, generating long-term social and cultural impacts as they have mined the deep seams of prejudice and division long embedded in Australian culture and society.

Regrettably, these seams of prejudice and division are easily accessed by those who might wish to exploit them to their political or commercial advantage. And there is quite a bit for them to work with. Australia has a racialist history of colonial settlement that is yet to be comprehensively acknowledged or its parties properly reconciled; it has lived through repeated phases of stigmatising immigrant communities perceived as insufficiently grateful or poorly assimilated; and even now it is dogged by a residual but stubborn resistance to implementing policies aimed at achieving gender equality in the workplace and elsewhere. The nation's ability to move beyond such attitudes has been actively impeded by the continuing influence of what remains of Australia's historical anti-intellectualism, the populist suspicion of progressive opinion and ideas, and the self-interested machinations of the nation's political class.

As they have engaged with the culture wars, participants in political debate and public commentary have regularly sliced

Australia up into opposing sociocultural orientations, ethnic, sexual or gender identities, and political interests. Some of this slicing has been straightforwardly cynical. This is exemplified by the opportunistic rhetorical invention of political categories deemed likely to resonate with targeted segments of the electorate – 'lifters not leaners', for instance. But other slices call up attitudes that are deeply embedded within Australian society and culture, and within entrenched fault lines of prejudice and intolerance. Racial prejudice has been regularly exploited, mostly via dog whistling, but sometimes deployed openly in the cultural battle against progressive ideas. Examples include the myths about Indigenous communities getting rich on welfare, the framing of Muslim asylum seekers as terrorists, and Peter Dutton's beat-up about African 'gangs' on the rampage in Melbourne. There is a class dimension to the culture wars as well. Australia's fabled egalitarianism doesn't seem to have limited the apparently endless political capital that can be earned by stigmatising the poor, the unemployed and the disabled as undeserving supplicants for 'excessive government handouts'.

This sociocultural battle has been going on since (at least) Prime Minister Howard engaged with what was initially an internal debate between Australian historians over their interpretation of Australia's colonial past. Disputing accounts that sought to recover the racialist origins of that history of settlement, Howard took up a public crusade against what he described as the 'black armband' version of Australian history.[28] On other fronts in which the definition of the national culture became politicised, Howard campaigned against the concept of multiculturalism, and against making a national apology to Indigenous Australians and the Stolen Generations.[29] An academic debate within the humanities disciplines about theories of postmodernism joined the list in the late 1990s as yet another elite idea characterised as posing an existential threat to Australian society.[30] These issues, along with the treatment of asylum seekers, gay marriage, climate change and environmentalism, were bundled up as 'politically correct' or 'woke', elite-driven, and thus 'fundamentally out of step with public concerns'.[31]

There was some hope that the election of the Rudd government would bring the culture wars to an end, but Rudd's wary 'me-too-ism' on some of these issues (asylum seekers, for instance) put paid to that. Jim George and Kim Huynh, in their analysis of the culture wars, argue that the Howard phase was merely one part of a longer, and continuing, history.[32] As the succeeding years have demonstrated, some of the more powerful conservative forces in Australia, following their role models in the United States, have turned out to be experts in 'the art of inventing an enemy', turning their attention to feminism, queer theory, gender and sexual identity.[33]

The actual content of the various versions of the culture wars, like the choice of target, depends upon the political circumstances of the time. Taken together, however, they have amounted to a cynical and opportunistic program of social division, which has exploited, and indeed exacerbated, fissures in the social fabric in order to secure political power. This has had an impact at the social and cultural level, of course: that is, upon many Australians' experience of their connection to the nation, and their sense of legitimacy and inclusion. At the political and strategic level, however, the culture wars have seriously, even disastrously, impacted on Australia's ability to respond in a timely, productive and well-informed manner to decades of social, cultural, technological and environmental change.

Consequently, this has been a difficult period for the imagining of a national community with which we might all choose to identify, and within which all Australians might feel acknowledged and included. The culture wars were, and indeed continue to be, a program of political resistance to social and cultural change. They were instigated to obstruct and forestall, by whatever means required, any likely reconfiguration of the existing asymmetries of power and influence, as well as any significant redistribution of resources and opportunity. The culture wars were especially focused on discrediting those arguing for social justice, while they shored up support for the continuing transfer of the nation's wealth from personal incomes to corporate profits. Constructing a vibrant culture was never a priority for the culture warriors, nor was building an inclusive and resilient national community.

As Australians face the legion of problems that have accrued over these decades, they are left to deal with that legacy – and with the task of turning it around. As suggested by the epigraph at the head of this chapter, this is not just a political task. It is also a social and cultural challenge, the reconstruction of the national imagination.

Nationing and cultural policy

How, then, might we approach a renewed sociocultural project of nation-building in the current conjuncture? It might help to revisit Australia's history of state and federal cultural policy agendas implemented over the 1970s, 1980s and into the 1990s, which addressed, informed and nurtured the national imagination, and thus helped to build the national community. The generative power of cultural policy to make a nation has been disregarded and neglected over the last two decades, however, and it is time that we were reminded of its substantial positive potential.

In 2018, with my colleagues David Rowe, a sociologist, and Emma Waterton, a cultural geographer, I co-edited a collection of academic essays entitled *Making Culture: Commercialisation, transnationalism and the state of 'nationing' in contemporary Australia.* The aim of the book was to examine recent shifts in the 'making' of our national culture, by focusing on changes in the deployment of cultural policy in Australia in the decades following the Keating government's *Creative Nation* policy statement of 1994.[34] Within *Creative Nation*, cultural policy was foregrounded as a central pillar for planning a project of nation formation. Since the period of the Howard government, however, the importance of culture to the framing of national policy initiatives has diminished under the pressure of more economistic and commercialising political imperatives. Over time, the approach taken in *Creative Nation* gave way to a policy framework that viewed the state of the national culture much more narrowly and instrumentally: that is, primarily 'as an object of industry policy'.[35]

Our book was interested in the uneven but nonetheless incremental withdrawal from the policy approach we refer to as 'nationing' – the objective of developing a national culture through the deployment of cultural policy.[36] *Creative Nation* exemplified this approach; it endowed cultural policy with the same degree of importance as social policy.[37] Cultural policy was positioned as fundamental to the creation and maintenance of a distinctive national culture, a coherent and functioning democratic society, and an inclusive national identity. Notably, too, *Creative Nation*'s version of culture broke with more traditional, elite and restricted definitions of culture by including popular cultural forms such as popular music as central to its purview. In *Creative Nation*, the formation of an inclusive national culture, with which all citizens might identify in their own various ways, and which (significantly, I think) gave them 'enjoyment and pleasure', was promoted as a desirable end in itself – the perfect model of a public good.

Drawing much of its strength from the cultural nationalism

that had been so powerful an influence during the period of the Hawke government, *Creative Nation* also reflected ideas that had significant international currency at the time. Projects of nation formation around the world, particularly in settler-colonial societies such as Australia's, had recognised the value of actively working towards the 'establishment of an inclusive national identity and a sense of belonging as a means of cohering diverse ethnic, racial, political and cultural elements into a functioning, modern and largely, but not exclusively, democratic nation-state'.[38] The cultural construction of national identity, then, was not just an ancillary to more material projects of nation-building; rather, it was a fundamental strategy to underpin the social viability of the nation-state. The focus of such a program was not just upon cultural enrichment or the modernisation of civil society – although it certainly dealt with both those objectives. More importantly for our purposes here, it was also focused upon building social and cultural bonds with the community as a means of regenerating an engagement with national identities and strengthening public forms of mutual obligation and responsibility.

Of course, over this period it was not only the Commonwealth government which invested in the production of culture. State governments were also highly significant actors – particularly in film production (especially in New South Wales, Victoria and South Australia) and popular music (Victoria led the way here).

I was personally involved, serving four years as chair of the Arts Advisory Committee for the Queensland government during the mid-1990s, when the Goss government (1989–1996) set about the task of renovating Queensland culturally, socially and politically. One of the key ways in which it approached this task was through investment in the arts and cultural organisations, something in which the previous National Party administrations had shown little interest during their twenty-one years in power. The Arts

Advisory Committee was the main source of policy advice to the premier, it designed and managed the expansion of an arts grants and subvention program, and it oversaw the budgets for the statutory bodies such as the state opera and the state theatre company.

Over its six years in office, the Goss government set up what became a highly successful Queensland Writers Centre, and extended its arts grants and support programs to include small and innovative performance arts companies as well as popular musicians seeking funds to produce CDs or go on tour. It forced hidebound major arts institutions such as the Queensland Opera to get out of Brisbane and take their work to the regions. The committee's grants programs supported regional museums and galleries, as well as community arts organisations. These were highly productive strategies for Australia's most decentralised state. The influence of the Goss government's suite of cultural policies played a major role in unravelling the conservative legacy of the Bjelke-Petersen regime and kick-starting the reinvention of the state's cultures and identity.

At the national level, the effect of such programs has been profound and long-lasting. This becomes apparent if one considers the importance of the imagined experience of national belonging that has been created, amplified, diversified and shared in the past, through the outcomes of some of these earlier cultural policy initiatives. This is another long list, but it demonstrates just how fundamental these initiatives have been as contributions to the construction of our imagined community – and to the style in which it has been imagined.

The 1970s saw the state and federal government-funded revival of the Australian film industry, the establishment of the SBS, the launching of youth music station Triple J, the establishment of the Australia Council, and the ramping-up of minimum local content standards (from 2 per cent to 20 per cent in 1976) as a basic support mechanism for local music on radio.

In the 1980s, there was a sustained period of highly successful investment by state and federal governments in the development of the Australian popular music industry and its marketing overseas, in the expansion of a popular and internationalising film industry, and in Australian-produced drama for television, which resulted in a boom in quality television miniseries.

Over the 1990s, there was increased public funding and recognition for community arts, heritage and independent theatre companies, as well as revised local content regulations for television. The federal anti-siphoning regulations, which limited the establishment of pay TV monopolies over television content of national importance (mostly major sporting events) were initially introduced in the 1990s and have continued, with some pauses and modifications, to the present.

If we cast our eyes further forward, it is perhaps telling that it becomes more difficult to cite initiatives of equivalent importance in the 2000s, as cultural policy began to slide from view, but the establishment of NITV within SBS as a free-to-air channel in 2012 stands out as one major cultural and political landmark.

Ricketson and Mullins suggest that one way to understand the cultural value of the ABC is to try to imagine what Australia would be like without it. That comment could equally be made about any one of these components of our national culture; it reminds us that each, in its own way, has helped to 'make' Australia. Try imagining an Australia without any of its own local drama productions for television and film, without its own popular music heroes and performance venues, without an independent theatre or comedy sector, or without its own literature. When we consider our personally preferred moments from such sectors, their distinctiveness and character comes clearly into the picture.

Think, for instance, of the film careers of Bryan Brown or Rachel Griffiths, the performances of bands such as the Divinyls or Midnight Oil, or the comedy produced by Shaun Micallef or Hannah Gadsby.

The cultural effect of engagement with the products of this sector can resonate for years after the actual event. In his recent article on the twenty-fifth anniversary of the release of *The Castle*, for instance, Russell Marks notes how firmly entrenched the film's one-liners have become within our national lexicon ('it's the vibe', 'tell 'em they're dreaming'), and emphasises what these 'can tell us about Australia'.[39] We risk losing sight of these kinds of value as policy makers have moved on to the prioritising of economic development in a context where the making of culture has assumed secondary importance.[40]

That is definitely a risk we face now. Over the last decade and more, in addition to some of the institutional depredations outlined earlier, there have been successive waves of deregulation and disinvestment in cultural institutions dealing with film, literature, broadcasting, conservation and heritage, performing arts, community arts, visual arts, and most of the collection and preservation sector (galleries, museums and libraries). The National Library, for instance, is now facing a bill of almost $87 million to replace infrastructure that is crumbling as a result of years of underfunding and neglect.[41] What remains of cultural policy is now framed around the notion that cultural activities should demonstrate their value in the marketplace and seek commercial viability rather than rely on continued government subvention.[42] Heritage and conservation organisations, for instance, increasingly depend on integrating their activities with those tourism industries focused on commodifying and marketing Australian culture rather than making it. This is yet another case where the choices involved in managing government investment in a public good or a public utility are being outsourced to the market.[43]

This tendency has prompted some to call for the development of an alternative policy framework: for developing a 'cultural economy', in which the economy works for the culture rather than the other way around.[44] This is more or less what *Creative Nation* set out to do, and it still offers us a credible model for developing strategies in the future.

That is not where we are at the moment, however. Even with the 2022 change in the federal government, there is no standalone ministry for culture; responsibility for the arts is tacked on to a long list of responsibilities for the Labor party's leader of the House of Representatives, Tony Burke. Burke, to be fair, has quickly taken the positive step of developing a National Cultural Policy – quite a task, given the running-down of the sector in recent years, but welcome just the same. It seems unlikely, however, to significantly modify the prevailing industry-oriented approach. For his part, the opposition leader, Peter Dutton, forgot to include his shadow minister for the arts in the announcement of his first shadow cabinet in May 2022.

While all of this may seem quite a depressing scenario, it is important to point out that it would not take much to turn it around. (After all, the Goss government managed to do it for Queensland in six years.) The current state of cultural policy, and the degree to which the Commonwealth is interested in the making of culture, are consequences of political choices. All that is required to revive a more progressive approach to the task of nationing is the political will to do so.

In addition to Tony Burke's National Cultural Policy, there are signs of the emergence of that political will at the state and federal level. With the New South Wales government recognising the need for a substantial cultural policy for rebuilding the distinctive cultures of the communities in Sydney, rather than merely a tourism campaign, and with other initiatives occurring at the state and regional levels elsewhere, we may be seeing a revival of political interest in the nation-forming and community-building capacities of cultural policy. It would certainly be a profitable direction for the country to explore as we move on from a thirty-year masterclass in how to deconstruct a nation, and begin to discover ways of putting it back together again.

CONCLUSION

Somewhere in here, there is a better country trying to get out

Around the time the ALP flirted with electoral suicide during the 2022 federal election campaign by going public with an acrimonious internal dispute about the party's treatment of the late senator Kimberley Kitching, Jacqueline Maley wrote a column for *The Sydney Morning Herald* which suggested that perhaps, at the bottom of all of this, there is something peculiar about politicians.

'British journalist Jeremy Paxman has a theory that politicians are simply a different class of people to the rest of us,' she wrote. Citing some recent and bitter internal factional wrangles within both major parties, she suggested there might be something to this theory:

> Ordinary people don't usually carry bitter enmities with them for decades. Most ordinary people don't despise their colleagues and connive to undermine them. They don't hate the people in their team more than the people they're supposed to be playing against. They don't have their funerals dominated by the conflicts

they fought in their professional lives, and they don't take members of their own organisation to court, and then appeal, and then appeal again.[1]

It certainly has its attractions, this idea. However, we are the ones who elect such people – and we do so repeatedly.

Political commentator Sean Kelly made a cogent point at the end of his 2021 book on Scott Morrison, written at a time when it seemed increasingly that Australians had had enough of Morrison and the style of politics he exemplified. 'If [Morrison] loses [the election],' Kelly wrote, 'we will likely tell ourselves that his failures as prime minister were his own, and that they have nothing at all to say about the rest of us.'[2] Kelly's implication, of course, is that actually it has a lot to do with the rest of us.

Morrison's government was the product of a political culture which has been not only tolerated by most Australians, but also vigorously promoted and exploited by many of those who could have chosen to do otherwise. Both the Abbott and Morrison governments were actively enabled by their supporters in the Murdoch media, by the powerful 'friends' whose enterprises the government privileged (notwithstanding the cost to the national interest), by the deep reservoir of regressive attitudes feeding into the culture wars, and by a complicit political class that had lost its moral compass as it became desensitised to the degraded political culture that had created it.[3]

Much of this environment remains unchanged. There is nothing to stop this feckless mode of governing or some further version of hyper-partisan populism from returning in the future. Indeed, at the time of writing, the approach the Coalition has taken to its role in opposition indicates that its members don't intend to renounce any of what they did in government, how they went about it or whose interests they served. Their fixation on destroying Labor, rather than improving policy in the national interest, continues. As for the incoming Labor government, after only four weeks in power its leaders had already chosen to deny they had backflipped by reversing their position on the expiry of the Covid support payment for casual workers, after first pretending that this was all down to the previous government and it was nothing to do with them. Depressingly familiar, this disingenuous set of moves was straight out of the political playbook of the Morrison government.

While certainly welcome and overdue, it is clear that the modest change in Australia's direction reflected in the 2022 election results will not develop momentum for a more substantial correction unless Australia can do much more to harness its better potential – that is, what can be done by 'the rest of us' to turn things around. Fortunately, however, there are signs – emanating, in particular, from beyond the boundaries of the political class – which encourage some faith in the power of that potential and the possibility of its realisation.

Curing the body politic

In his compelling account of the 'making of America's fury' over the last three decades, *Wildland*, Evan Osnos discusses the 'antibodies' to America's ills that were responsible for Trump's eventual defeat in the last election:

> The backlash to Trump was not only a rebuttal to the politics of exclusion and fear and dominance; it was also a war on the dogma of starving a government to the point of dysfunction; it was a declaration of hope that a well-run government could be a unifying force. That rebuttal, from across American life, felt

analogous to a biological process – antibodies converging on an illness in the body politic, a battle to suppress the culture of 'thoughts and prayers', white supremacy, the corruption of democracy, and the sheer force of cynicism.[4]

Although we can't predict what long-term influence the teal independents might have on the federal Labor government's program of legislation, it is possible, when viewed in conjunction with the electorate's evident disaffection with the major parties, that they will constitute something like an Australian strain of these antibodies 'converging on an illness in the body politic'. At the very least, the election of so many independent candidates does challenge the prospect of 'politics as usual', and so over time might provide the basis for a more comprehensive political reset for the nation in the future.

To appropriate Julia Gillard's reported analysis of the role of gender in her political downfall, while the fact that the teals were all women is not everything, neither is it nothing. After all, they belong to the 51 per cent of Australians who are entitled to believe that their concerns have been given scant attention by state and federal governments, even though these concerns have been around for years. They include the failure to seriously address the gender pay gap, to understand the importance of affordable childcare to women wanting to return to the workforce, to fix the deplorable levels of remuneration in industries where women dominate, and to redress the inadequate response to the rising incidence of sexual violence and sexual harassment in the workplace, in the home and on the street. Men's domination of the political class and the skewed gender make-up of our parliament helped to make the teals' case for them: simply by being women, they represented a visible challenge to the status quo.

Further, by refusing party alignment, they repudiated another element of the status quo: the hyper-partisan prosecution of party lines within our political culture. Although climate change, improved funding for the 'caring' industries and integrity in government were their most prominent campaign issues, the teals also implicitly stood for the majority of women, who, pollsters reveal, have had enough of these men's lack of interest in women's concerns, and their resistance to achieving gender equality and ensuring women's safety. What the teals' success also reflects, however, is the breaking of a wave of social and cultural change over 2019–2022 in which women's struggles over these issues achieved heightened public visibility and support.

The ABC TV *Four Corners* report 'Inside the Canberra Bubble', broadcast in November 2020, examined the workplace culture within the federal parliament by focusing on accusations of sexual misconduct against Coalition government ministers Christian Porter and Alan Tudge. It was followed shortly after, in early 2021, by the explosive allegations that parliamentary aide Brittany Higgins had been raped by a fellow staffer in a parliamentary office just down the hall from the prime minister's. The government's reaction was first to cover it up, and then to obfuscate over who knew what and when, and what actions were taken as a consequence. The continuing prevarication, as well as the establishment of two internal reviews aimed at forestalling questions from the media, only served to fuel the anger of women, who naturally understood the purpose of such strategies. The series of 'Enough Is Enough' marches that followed in 2021 were powerful and widely reported expressions of that anger. Although this particular movement lost momentum over time, it had succeeded in generating public awareness of, and a sustained concern about, the Coalition government's failure to acknowledge women's concerns.

Pressure related to the Coalition's growing 'women problem' built up over 2021 and into 2022. In an attempt to hose it down, the

Respect@Work report by sex discrimination commissioner Kate Jenkins, which had been buried by the Coalition government for two years after its completion, was exhumed for tabling in 2022.[5] Soon after the Labor government came to power, it committed to implementing the report's recommendations in full. That's a positive step, of course, but it is clear that this won't be the end of the matter. Much more in these areas of policy remains to be done.

The need for action is supported by research and information coming not only from government and academic researchers but also from independent think tanks, from social services agencies and from some of the charities that had been left to fill the gaping holes in government services for women. The 2022 report by the Workplace Gender Equality Agency (WGEA) is just one example of such research; it found that the average pay gap between men and women in Australia currently stood at 13.6 per cent.[6] Surprising to some, but not at all to those who have been paying closer attention, the report formed just one part of the growing body of evidence that is now being used to place these issues in front of the public.

In this area, as in so many others, the pace of social and cultural change has run far in advance of the response from our political institutions. The last three years, in particular, have seen a dramatic increase in the intensity of the public's interest in gender issues, as part of what Annabel Crabb has described as a 'new era of attentiveness to women's experience'.[7] Fuelled by the outrage that built up around the allegations made by Brittany Higgins, this attentiveness reached a new level of prominence in media debate over 2021. That year, SBS screened its documentary series based on Jess Hill's 2019 book, *See What You Made Me Do*, a chilling analysis of domestic violence in Australia.[8] Louise Milligan, the ABC journalist responsible for

'Inside the Canberra Bubble', published her book *Witness: An investigation into the brutal cost of seeking justice*, a personal account of how the Australian court systems discriminate against women.[9] Historian and ABC presenter Julia Baird, responding to the shift in the zeitgeist, produced a revised and updated version of her 2004 book, *Media Tarts: How the Australian press frames female politicians*, in which she issued a call for action: '[T]here is no more time for patience,' she said, 'we have all the evidence we need.'[10] Adding to that body of evidence, former federal Labor minister Kate Ellis published her own research into what it is to be a female politician, *Sex, Lies and Question Time*, substantiating the 'perception ... that politics is hostile to women's interests, women's needs and women's lives'.[11]

Four young women, in particular, had substantial impact not only on informing such public perceptions but also upon policy development and sexual consent legislation across the nation. Two women who were survivors of sexual assault and sexual abuse, Saxon Mullins and Grace Tame, became prominent and influential advocates for change.

In 2021, Mullins, the director of Rape and Sexual Assault Research and Advocacy (RASARA), and a recipient of the Australian Human Rights Commission's 2018 Young People Human Rights Medal, who had courageously built upon her exposure through a 2018 *Four Corners* story by Louise Milligan, 'I Am That Girl', led a radical overhaul of New South Wales's sexual assault laws.

Grace Tame, an exceptionally steely and charismatic woman, became such a powerful advocate for survivors of sexual abuse that she was named Tasmania's Australian of the Year in 2020 and the Commonwealth's Australian of the Year in 2021. Tame attracted widespread attention (both positive and negative, but that's the territory) for her uncompromising campaign for social, cultural and legal change around Australia's dealing with women's and children's rights.

Graduate student Chanel Contos, responding to what she had learned from the research for her thesis, launched an online campaign that revealed shocking levels of sexual assault and sexual abuse among school-age children and teenagers. This campaign eventually led to an historic agreement between the state and territory education ministers to make sexual consent education a compulsory component in their schools' curriculum.

And, finally, there was Brittany Higgins, whose brave and measured prosecution of her allegations of sexual assault within Parliament House has been the catalyst for heightened public concern about the toxic and misogynistic workplace culture tolerated by our nation's leaders.

In a parallel development, young Indigenous women have also had heightened visibility in public debates. In her updated and revised edition of *Sister Girl*, Jackie Huggins highlights the emergence of a cadre of young, well-educated, forthright and articulate Indigenous women taking on positions of political, corporate, social and cultural leadership.[12] Regular viewers of ABC TV's *The Drum* will have seen a number of these impressive young women, and it is to be hoped that they represent a significant shift in the racial and gendered topography of Australia's political and cultural landscape.

There are other signs of such a shift, as well, with politics at last perhaps starting to catch up with the culture in a crucial area of national debate. Anthony Albanese's speech claiming victory in the 2022 election gave historic prominence to his party's commitment to accepting the Uluru Statement from the Heart. Regrettably, it is true, this was not linked to addressing the longer-term public policy and human rights failures identified in the *Closing the Gap* report, but it was at the very least a welcome move towards a more respectful engagement with Indigenous Australians. At the time of writing, however, we don't have bipartisan political support for an Indigenous Voice to Parliament, and there has been some softening of public support since the ABC's Vote Compass Survey of May 2022 found that 73 per cent of Australians were in favour.[13] Nonetheless, the strong public commitment from major corporations such as Wesfarmers and BHP, from sporting bodies such as the AFL, from the big four banks, and from all state premiers, is significant.

These commitments are consistent with a pattern of shifts in public opinion which encourage the view that a more genuine embrace of Australia's Indigenous histories may be underway. In July 2022, the New South Wales government announced that it would be replacing the state flag on the Sydney Harbour Bridge with the Aboriginal flag. Indigenous faces on our television and movie screens have increased in number in recent years, to the extent that their representation in television drama, for example, is now at a higher percentage than their proportion of the population.[14] The role of NITV in the development of an Indigenous screen production sector has helped to make it 'a force to be reckoned with', while the popular success of an Indigenous feel-good movie such as *The Sapphires* (2012), along with the critical success of high-end television drama such as *Redfern Now!* (2012–2013) and *Cleverman* (2016–2017), has taken Indigenous film and television productions into the mainstream.[15] Although it may seem to some an unlikely location for progressive cultural leadership on race, the National Rugby League (NRL), with its many Indigenous players, has had a long-term commitment to publicly celebrating Indigenous culture. The NRL's annual Indigenous Round has become an iconic inclusion in the code's national calendar.

A further crucial area of political debate where progressive popular opinion has been pushing back against political resistance is in relation to climate change and environmental protection.

Climate change was a key issue for voters in the last federal election, and public support for greater action continues to grow. The Lowy Institute's *Climate Poll 2021* found that 60 per cent of Australians surveyed believed that global warming was a 'serious and pressing problem', while 74 per cent believed that taking further action on climate change 'will outweigh the cost'.[16] A year later, *The Ipsos Climate Change Report 2022* told us that 83 per cent of Australians are concerned about climate change, with 70 per cent believing that Australia was already being affected (in 2011, that figure was 56 per cent).[17]

These percentages are not surprising, given the frequency with which extreme natural disaster events have hit the country over recent years. What continues to surprise, unfortunately, is the obduracy of the political resistance to what the science tells us, to developing strategies for adaptation and recovery, and to taking timely and decisive action to expedite the transition from fossil fuels to renewable sources of energy.

There is no shortage of activism, research and community calls for action, but stalled government policy on climate change has been one of the great failures of Australia's political class in the modern era. Heavily indebted to the sponsorship of what journalist Marian Wilkinson calls 'the carbon club',[18] intimidated by the political muscle the mining industry lobby exercised in its successful targeting of the Rudd government, and happy to be cheered on by the climate deniers in the Murdoch media, they have let Australia down. The 'rest of us' have done our best to be heard, but progress has been slow and limited. At the same time, alarming progress reports on the state of the environment turn up with wearying regularity. Upon taking office in mid-2022, environment minister Tanya Plibersek uncovered a *State of the Environment* report so 'shocking' that it had been held back from release by the previous government prior to the election.[19]

This is a field of policy where, regrettably, the struggles for a better Australia are yet to achieve the influence required to deliver the policy changes that are needed. The better Australia is certainly trying to break through to 'cure the body politic', but the combined power of a regressive political ideology, an often hostile media commentariat and significant vested commercial interests has so far generated stiff resistance. While there have been positive policy initiatives from various state governments, at the federal level there is still caution, deferral and indecision.

Such hesitancy is not unique to this issue. Rather, it is among the consequences of Australian politicians' entrenched conviction that the electorate is loath to countenance any change that might have negative consequences for the status quo. Inaction on climate change, in particular, seems also to be influenced by another factor that haunts the politicians of both major parties: that is, fear of doing anything which might unleash the ferocity of the Murdoch media.

More significantly, perhaps, and at the level of transactional politics, there are still active political battlelines within the current federal parliament that stand in the way of a conclusive resolution of the debate over climate policy. The bitter political rivalry between the Greens and Labor is set to continue. Furthermore, Labor is not particularly inclined to do any deals on legislation which might enhance the public's sense that the teals can be an effective force for good policy. These obstacles will continue to limit the chances of a bipartisan commitment to addressing emissions control, a revised energy policy, strategies for adaptation or a fully developed plan for protecting the natural environment. Possibly the best we can hope for over the medium term is a series of modest resets of the political dial, with the further necessary battles once again deferred into the future.

The people's nation

When we look beyond the world of politics and the machinations of the political class, it is not so difficult to find examples of what a better version of our nation looks like. Australia's popular culture still regularly turns up reminders of the iconoclasm, invention and ingenuity that have long fed into mythologies of the national character and that continue to deliver many of our popular pleasures. The gleeful outburst of satire produced by our cartoonists, and television shows such as Micallef's *Mad as Hell,* in response to the Morrison 'fistful of ministries' revelations, comes to mind here. Or the experience of listening to 'Rampaging' Roy Slaven and HG Nelson riff for close to an hour on radio about the serendipity of the NRL's Canterbury Bulldogs finding themselves a corporate sponsor with the name Sydney Tools. Or watching the extraordinary response of the nation's children (and many of their parents) to *Bluey.*

There are regular signs of progressive change and expanding opportunity within the broader culture, too. We now have successful women's competitions in all the major football codes, for instance, and in November 2021 the national women's soccer team, the Matildas, attracted more than 36,000 fans to watch them play at Stadium Australia in Sydney. In cricket, a crowd of 86,000 turned out to watch Australia play India in the final of the Women's T20 World Cup at the MCG in 2020. Recent choices for Australian of the Year, Grace Tame (2021) and Dylan Alcott (2022), recognised the value of activism on gender issues and the necessity for a genuine commitment to the inclusion of Australians with a disability.

If television has lost some of its power as a mass medium, it still offers us a unique window through which we can see the signs of social and cultural change. It does not simply reflect society, but the distance between television and everyday life has been steadily decreasing for years – partly, but not only, due to the 'realities' constructed by reality TV. While what we see on television may be only the tip of the social iceberg – it is just the bit that's visible – it can tell us much about how our culture sees itself, and how that might be changing. It has taken a long time for the cultural diversity of the Australian community to be accurately represented in Australian television, but we seem at last to be approaching a tipping point. Not only has the representation of Indigenous Australians become more common on screen, but other forms of ethnic and cultural diversity have as well. We can see, for instance, a more recognisable, culturally diverse and inclusive version of Australia in Channel Ten's popular cooking contest *MasterChef* (2009–). Unlike some of the other programs competing in the reality TV/gameshow space, the contestants on *MasterChef* are not looking to become media celebrities; they want to become successful chefs. The series does not cast for personal conflict between contestants – as its main competitor, Channel Seven's *My Kitchen Rules*, does (and as do most reality TV/gameshow hybrids). *MasterChef* is definitively not a narcissistic, individualist, hyper-competitive product of neoliberalism. Indeed, over its first fourteen seasons, the program is remarkable for the generosity and sense of community that builds up among the contestants.

MasterChef contestants are chosen for their talent and ability – these are skilled and dedicated cooks rather than the media-savvy, 'up-for-it' extroverts offered up as performative spectacles who feature across most reality-TV franchises. The process to which *MasterChef* participants submit themselves is long (up to three months, with five episodes per week), unforgiving and personally demanding. They deserve respect, and they are given it by the program hosts and judges.

Notably, the contestants, when we see them lined up together, actually look like contemporary Australia. They exhibit the full range of diversity Australians encounter every day – cultural, ethnic, generational, gendered and sexual. Furthermore, this diversity extends to the cooking. Local and regional food traditions are especially honoured, no matter where they come from (the international cuisines most often featured are those most common within the broader community, Asian and Italian, but they are not the only ones). And although by the time we reach the 'finale' this diversity of food traditions is funnelled into the more narrow remit of a set task that comes from Western fine dining (usually a ridiculously complex dessert), there can be no doubting *MasterChef*'s commitment to cultural diversity.

Another take on cultural diversity, less mainstream and more challenging, comes from ABC TV's *Love on the Spectrum* (2019–2021). While formatted as a dating show and thus also belonging within the genre of reality TV, this is actually more like a documentary series. It follows seven young adults, all on the autism spectrum, as they are coached through a series of dates with the hope of finding a romantic partner. This is tricky territory, of course, and it has attracted some debate over how well the producers navigate their way through it. However, *Love on the Spectrum* documents with sensitivity and affection the personal and social difficulties facing people with autism while they try to find a partner. The considerable social value of the program lies in the fact that it has taken on the task of improving the public's understanding of what it is to live with autism, in order to remove some of the barriers that separate people with disabilities from the rest of the community.

Love on the Spectrum has been a success, with a third series reportedly being considered. The dynamics of that success were on view when the 'ordinary people' who watch television for Channel Ten's *Gogglebox* were shown *Love on the Spectrum*.[20]

Gogglebox is not a place where television can expect any favours. Indeed, the appeal of the show lies in its unique combination of enthusiasm for the pleasures of watching television with its default scepticism about the medium and its products. This was an interesting test, then, of how well *Love on the Spectrum* did its job for the average (that is, not just the ABC) viewer.

Initially, the *Gogglebox*-ers regarded the show as a curiosity. However, the honesty and vulnerability of the *Love on the Spectrum* characters quickly drew the *Gogglebox*-ers into their world and to a strongly supportive engagement with them. In the end, theirs was not a response to people with disabilities, although they were certainly touched by the nature of the difficulties the characters' autism presented. Rather, the *Gogglebox* viewers responded to them as relatable human beings, who were 'like everyone else' in that they 'deserved love'. (One pair were so smitten with 'Michael', they said he should be cast as the next *Bachelor*.) By the time they got around to watching the dates unfold, the viewers were fully committed – vigorously barracking for their character, willing it to work out and groaning in sympathy when it didn't.

As entertainment, *Love on the Spectrum* worked for the *Gogglebox*-ers because it was heartwarming, empathic and insightful, while maintaining the narrative and romantic hooks of the dating-show format: will the couples connect or not? As a contribution to a better Australia, it did just what it set out to do: it rescued a category of Australians from ignorance and misunderstanding, thereby reactivating their membership within the broader community.

There are also moments when ordinary people's membership of the national community becomes dramatically visible. These are typically moments of national celebration or solidarity, when substantial public gatherings of Australians behave as enthusiastic contributors to something larger than themselves. The Fire Fight

Australia concert for national bushfire relief, staged at Sydney's ANZ Stadium on 16 February 2020, is one such occasion. The event raised $9 million for the victims of the Black Summer fires of 2019–2020, and expressed the public's appreciation of the heroism of those who fought the fires. As many as 75,000 people attended the concert, which was screened live on free-to-air television. It closed with a rousing rendition of Australia's 'unofficial national anthem', 'You're the Voice', John Farnham sharing the vocals with Olivia Newton-John and Indigenous singer Mitch Tambo. A bunch of firies, in their high-vis vests, lined up across the stage to wave to the crowd, barely leaving room for Farnham's bagpipers. In a context framed by public criticism of government inaction on the one hand, and admiration of the resilience and selflessness of the community on the other, this event reminded us of the continuing presence of a better nation.

Such events can do more than just reaffirm our membership to the national community, however. They can also be transformative, generating public reflection on, and debate about, the things we value. The example I want to focus on here is the commemoration of the life of former Australian cricketer Shane Warne.

Warne died unexpectedly in 2022 at the age of fifty-two, his death shocking the nation and the international cricket world. Media coverage of his passing was extensive. The tabloid newspapers, which had previously been shameless in their exploitation of Warne's notoriety by sensationalising every one of his off-field adventures and misadventures, suddenly appeared to have discovered he was actually a person of whom the nation should be proud. Sydney's *Sunday Telegraph*, notable as among those responsible for turning Warne into a human headline, published a commemorative wraparound amounting to ten pages. The prime minister offered Warne's family a state funeral, but in the end they opted, fittingly, for a people's celebration of his life: a public memorial that was held at the Melbourne Cricket Ground on 30 March 2022.

This event was coupled with the renaming of the MCG's Great Southern Stand as the Shane Warne Stand. Interestingly, given our focus here, Warne's family rejected the official and traditional suggestion that the stand be called the SK Warne Stand, and insisted instead on the more vernacular Shane Warne Stand.

Warne's MCG memorial event was televised and screened live at primetime on every commercial network as well as the ABC. It featured panels of friends and colleagues talking about the cricket star and the man, as well as music from Elton John, Chris Martin and Ed Sheeran. A touching tribute from Warne's grieving children helped steer us away from the mass-mediated figure created by the tabloids, in order to focus on the kind of man he was to those who knew him best and on the lives he touched, many of them beyond the world of cricket. Some 2.5 million people watched the tribute on television in Australia, and more than 50,000 came to the MCG to watch it in person.

The ABC's current-affairs program *7.30* replayed an earlier Leigh Sales interview with Warne, which presented him as considerably more thoughtful and interesting than the person in the headlines, while Sales happily revealed her engaging fan-girl pleasure in being able to talk with him. Coincidentally, a documentary on Warne's career, *Shane*, had been released in January 2022, and its respectful representation of the player and the man disclosed dimensions to his life and his abilities that hadn't made the headlines. Out of all of this, and while he was clearly no saint, Warne stood confirmed not only as a national sporting hero for his extraordinary achievements on the cricket field, but also as a better and more complex man than the media had allowed him to be through his public life.

This was a national celebration, a public appreciation of the pleasure and pride this one man had generated for the nation, and a moment for the imagined community of the nation to gather together to acknowledge an inspiring and relatable image of itself. Certainly, there were some who regarded all of this as excessive – he was just a cricketer, after all. However, it is no small feat for one person to bring so much of the nation together in respect and admiration for achievements that were regarded as not just of that man, but of the nation.

It is at moments such as these, I argue, that the imagined community of the nation asserts its continued presence and its power, as it delivers the pleasures of belonging.

Fixing the shrinking nation

Let's return, finally, to the state of the nation's political culture and to the broader sociocultural malaise this book has focused upon – and to what might be done about it.

There is no shortage of suggestions about how Australia might address this situation. Contemporary commentators seize upon the daily modulations in the nation's political culture as triggers for updated diagnoses of the nation's ills and prescriptions for their treatment. Mostly, however, such prescriptions are to do with the political management of the economy rather than with the waves of sociocultural change we have examined in this book. These are not only economic issues, though. Australia has contracted a cultural condition that has social consequences – both specific and wide-ranging, immediate and long-term – for the nation. These can't continue to be ignored, and it is notable that a number of state governments have gradually recognised this fact. While their responses only represent the beginning of what needs to be done, they do at least take on the task of addressing some of the social issues previous federal governments have been slow to acknowledge – by, for instance, increasing subsidies for childcare, exploring new ways of improving the delivery of rural health, funding the construction of more social housing, and committing significant political capital to renewable energy sources.

There are examples, then, of what governments might do. The palpable sense that the state has failed its citizens, however, is going to take more than a political fix. Australians must be able to trust their governments. They need to believe that those charged with governing actually respect and are committed to the task they have been given: ensuring the wellbeing and security of all citizens.

Australia now faces a substantial rethinking of the role of the state – of what we actually want our governments to do. That, in turn, and as many now argue, will necessitate a reorientation of our political culture to reinstate the centrality of governments, rather than markets, in determining the quality, the character and the social viability of our society.[21] During the heyday of neoliberal economic policy, such a proposition would have been dismissed as heresy, but the pandemic has given us a reality check. That is why we are now hearing concerns about, for instance, the running-down of the public sector, the rise in inequality and disadvantage, the social consequences of gender inequity and the need for a public debate about just what kinds of services Australians want their governments to provide. Richard Denniss speaks for the mood of the moment when he says that it is time Australians asked this basic question: 'What kind of country do we want to build?' The asking of that question, of itself, implies that we can no longer pretend to leave such a decision to the market.[22]

This is a social, cultural and ethical question about what we believe is right, decent and necessary – not just what is 'affordable'. However, this question has rarely been asked in recent years. Instead, and although trickle-down economics has been discredited, public debate about political choices has continued to prioritise what might be good for the economy, rather than what might be good for the culture, the society or the nation – or, indeed, for the poor as well as the rich. Even now, and notwithstanding all we have learned over the period of the pandemic, the default position for so much of the political debate that occurs in the public sphere still involves the core assumption that what is good for business must always, necessarily, be good for the nation.

We have been provided with repeated demonstrations that this is a false assumption. As I write, an Australia Institute report is attracting widespread attention for its finding that increased corporate profits, not rising wages, are most responsible for driving up Australia's inflation.[23] Such a finding is explosive, blowing apart years of fiscal policy and government talking points from both sides of politics. Even putting it like that, though, draws some of its teeth, such that this finding may not be understood for what it actually means. What it actually means is that ordinary Australians are finding it harder to make ends meet because corporations have been using the disrupted economic environment as cover for their decision to raise prices and supercharge their own profits. This comes as no surprise to government, of course. We know now that successive governments have pursued a deliberate policy of supporting the maximising of profits while suppressing growth in wages, all justified by the claim that this was in line with the orthodox strategies for effectively curbing inflation.

Australians need to seriously examine the social and cultural outcomes of what our economy now does, and to ask if these are the outcomes we desire (and, if they are not, to set about changing what the economy does). We also need to ask ourselves some serious historical questions: just how did Australia get to the point of implicitly regarding the enrichment of an ever-diminishing fraction of the population as the primary purpose of the nation? Why have the rest of us tolerated that? Why have our governments facilitated it? And how do we now turn that around?

The first step is to stop thinking of the nation as reducible to the economy. There is more to it than that. Once we dethrone the economy from its position of political pre-eminence, we can focus our attention on the making of an inclusive culture, a cohesive community and a fair and just society. The neoliberals' fetishisation of the economy and faith in the market were sustained by the fact that most of the benefits they delivered went to those who were closest to, or had privileged access to, the sources of political power. From where we sit today, it is reasonable to suggest that the nation would have been better served by improving the conditions of everyday life for all Australians, by establishing a humane and accessible safety net for those who need it, and by properly investing in the services that its citizens expect and need from their government – in health, education and aged care, for instance. If such considerations had framed our experience of the last twenty years, it is likely we would be living in a very different nation to the one we inhabit today.

And we have had such a policy orientation before. It is worth remembering that Australia has a history of believing in the value of the nation-building mission, and in the importance of actively working towards the development of a rich, diverse, equitable and inclusive culture. Classifying the making of the national culture as a second-order issue – one of interest only to an elite, self-interested class fraction – has had regrettable long-term consequences.

Our record of setting out to create a just and equitable society, in which the most vulnerable were properly cared for, has been tarnished in recent decades as that objective has been side-lined. Rather than being regarded as a moral imperative fundamental to a civilised democratic society, the provision of adequate and effective social support systems for Australia's citizens was routinely framed as something that was (almost inherently) unaffordable. The ongoing cost to the government, we were told, was so far beyond our means that it would 'send a wrecking ball through the economy'. (Increasing JobSeeker would do this, it seems, but cutting taxes for the rich apparently would not.) Anything likely to endanger what those who benefited from it chose to call 'the economy' was not only vigorously attacked but also drawn into whatever culture war was underway at the time.

To our detriment, the political concentration on the economy failed to enliven the imagination of the national community, serving only to foster the instrumentalism and self-interested individualism which undermined a sense of belonging to the nation. Along the way, it created a downward spiral of deepening inequality and social division, ate away at the capacities of the state and diminished the quality of what many Australians have experienced as their way of life.

That's a tough diagnosis, perhaps, but we are not at the end of the story yet. Notwithstanding the continuing problems we have examined, there remain grounds for hope of improvement, of making progress in fixing the shrinking nation. Paul Keating is often quoted as saying that 'when you change the government, you change the country'. The establishment of effective and responsible political leadership, as Anthony Albanese appears to have understood, can be a major and positive step towards changing the country for the better. It has the potential of remaking the relation between the state and its citizens. If the role of our political leaders in cynically fomenting division has been among the crucial elements here – and in my view the prime ministerships of Abbott and Morrison could well be described in that way – then this is also the role that can be most easily turned around by a leader committed to hitting the 'off' switch on our bad politics.

The 2022 election results might be seen as hinting at a rebellion against the political culture this book has described. The support for the teals suggests that this rebellion was motivated in large part by the demand for a proper reckoning with climate change, for the establishment of proper mechanisms of integrity and accountability for government, and for a commitment to better resourcing the 'care industries'.

We can point to some positive outcomes from this. Each of those themes featured in the October 2022 federal budget, and the legislation for a federal integrity commission made it through parliament in the last sitting weeks of 2022. Gender equity in the workplace is to be addressed in legislation under consideration at the time of writing, and a greater investment in combating the epidemic of domestic violence is to be made. There has been some progress on addressing the profiteering on energy prices, although greater political courage will be required to do more. Climate change remains a polarising issue, regrettably, but there are some small steps towards dealing with it properly at the federal level, as well as more substantial interventions at the state level in New South Wales, Victoria and Queensland.

We have heard promises from Albanese of a 'kinder, gentler' political culture. There is little sign of that being matched by the federal opposition, though, so it is unlikely that the government will stick to it either. Nonetheless, there are still some indications that our politicians have not only got the message from a fed-up electorate, but are finding some elements of the courage required to respond to it. The federal treasurer, Jim Chalmers, has adopted the novel approach of being 'honest' with the electorate about the economic challenges in the future; this has been applauded as a positive step towards turning federal politics into the much-promised 'adult conversation'. Most interestingly, there are some indications that the ousting of the Morrison government constitutes something of a turning point in the tolerance that some in the media, and perhaps the public as well, have for the toxic politics that shaped the behaviour of that government.

A case in point is Errington and Van Onselen's recent book dealing with the Labor victory. While their 2021 book on Scott Morrison was certainly critical of him and of his government, they were also relatively circumspect in how they articulated this – presumably because there was no guarantee he would lose the election and they may have had to deal with him in the future. The latest book, in contrast, makes little attempt to disguise its contempt for Morrison, or for the political culture over which he presided.[24] The clarity of the electorate's expression of opinion may have emboldened the authors to say what they really think, and to stand up for a better version of politics.

The debacle surrounding former British prime minister Liz Truss's extraordinary attempt to retrofit neoliberal orthodoxies to the mess that is post-Johnson Britain has been widely regarded as a death blow to the ideology of trickle-down economics. Even 'the markets', it would seem, no longer buy this idea. While this at least encourages some hope that we have come to the end of this phase in our political history, the consequences of neoliberalism for our nation remain. The most concerning are the underpinnings of Australia's worrying pattern of rising inequality: the affordability crisis for housing, the stagnation of wages, the deterioration in the provision of support services to the needy, and the shift of the nation's wealth from personal incomes to corporate profits. There is also the effect of the stigmatisation of the recipients of welfare benefits, which was originally deployed as a means of politically nullifying their claims to entitlement but which has generated longstanding and destructive cultural and social consequences.

A lot to repair, then, and in many cases potentially expensive. In comparison to the situation in the United Kingdom, however, there is some appreciation of many of these issues in recent Australian state and federal budgets, and a significant stiffening of the political will to find ways to address them. The new federal industrial relations bill has the explicit intention of boosting wages, there has been increased funding for health and aged care within state budgets, and the Albanese government has committed to substantial investment aimed at reviving the capacities, performance and independence of the Australian public service. Much of this is slated to happen down the track, and will inevitably hit budgetary obstacles, but at least the importance of these issues is no longer being dismissed.

How to address them into the future brings us back to that core question: what kind of nation do Australians want to build? This, in turn, takes us into debates about how we can generate extra funding to resource the strategies required to deal with these problems. Journalist Jessica Irvine has raised an interesting proposition about how we might modify the tax system to that end. She suggests expanding the Medicare levy into a 'Care Services' levy to fund healthcare, childcare and aged care – starting at a rate of 0.5 per cent of taxable income for those on low incomes, rising to 5 per cent for those on the highest incomes.[25] Assessing the relative merits of this option resides outside my expertise, and is also outside the remit of this book, but the value of this proposition lies in its assumption that our governments need to take responsibility for improving the levels of wellbeing that all Australians can expect over their lifetimes.

Once we decide what kind of country we want, we have to actually do things to build it. Not just material things – housing, infrastructure and so on. We have to think about how we build a culture that is enriching and inclusive; about how we build communities that are resilient and cohesive; and about how we re-establish the ethical, moral and democratic baselines that enable the functioning of a just and equitable society. The process my co-authors and I described as nationing – beginning with the commitment to an explicit program for making culture – must be placed back in the foreground of such considerations. We can see in the popular culture around us that the raw materials for a lively and vibrant culture are still there. The people's nation may have shrunk but it hasn't disappeared. It will only flourish to its full potential, however, if all its members are recognised, validated and offered dignity and respect. A community like that can turn the shrinking nation around.

The Australian electorate is learning that governments can't build a nation by 'getting out of the way' and 'letting the market decide'. But if they are to play a significant role in the process of nationing, then we need the kind of government that we don't wish to get out of the way. A well-run and trusted government, representative of the whole community, transparent and responsive to a broadly informed idea of the national interest, and committed to the protection and wellbeing of its citizens, can be a unifying force. We have had such governments before in our history, and it is not too much to ask that we have them again.

Achieving that, however, will require a thorough and ongoing repudiation of the political culture that has delivered to us the shrinking nation that has been the subject of this book. We may have started that journey, but there's still a long way to go. We can, however, learn from what has gone wrong over the past two decades, and put that knowledge to work – raising the bar on what we demand from our political representatives, renovating the quality and integrity of our public culture, and generating social and cultural policy settings that facilitate the development of a more just and equitable society. There is much to be done, but also much we can do, to make this a better country for all of its citizens.

Author's note

This book was developed and written during a difficult period for Australians. For the communities where I live, in the Northern Rivers region of New South Wales, it has been especially difficult. 2019–20 brought the Black Summer bushfires, which burned rainforests and destroyed communities. The onset of Covid-19, and the lockdowns and border closures that came with it, carried particular hardships for rural border communities. For some in my region, such as those who were dependent upon health and hospital services they had previously accessed across the border in Queensland, the restrictions were potentially life-threatening. Supply chains for food and fuel are especially vulnerable in rural areas, and the supermarket shortages and delays for services were severe and lasting. And then came the 2022 floods – two massive waves of them, in February and March, that devastated the region. The local councils will never be able to afford to rebuild all the infrastructure that was destroyed, and the human consequences continue.

This was a testing time, then, in which it was hard not to reflect on the condition of our nation, the limits of our resilience, and the capacity and commitment of the state to support the security and wellbeing of all Australians. As it happens, I had been thinking about such things for some time before this. As a researcher and writer, I had been studying the conditions of our national culture and society, off and on, since the 1980s, and had maintained a long-term interest both in the changing formations of Australian nationalism and in the cultural policy settings aimed at building a national culture. In another sphere of engagement, as a senior academic researcher, I had been charged at various times with representing parts of the university sector, so I had considerable experience dealing with governments, both state and federal. This had taught me not to underestimate the extent of the obstacles confronting the ambition to deliver progressive change in service of the public good.

Consequently, I have watched the accelerating pace of social and cultural change over the last two decades with both a professional and a personal interest. From these twin perspectives, it was apparent that the evolving political culture in Australia was not serving us well – for all the reasons and in all the circumstances I have outlined in this book. For me personally – and, I believe, for many others – it was becoming harder to feel good about how my country was travelling.

This was an unsettling state of mind, and much at odds with the heady bursts of cultural nationalism I had enjoyed experiencing at other moments in our history. I remember the sense of cultural opportunity, of the cosmopolitanising and modernising momentums that built up in Australian culture and society during the two decades which followed the end of the Menzies era. At such times, Australia seemed like it was becoming more of its own place, more confident and open, in ways that made it feel bigger and better than it had been before. My experience of the last two decades has been, increasingly, the opposite of this.

As I believe many of us have found, our disaster-ridden experiences of the last three years have exposed just how thoroughly Australia – as a culture, as a society, as a nation – has been diminished over these decades. Most damningly, they revealed how poorly we have been served by short-sighted and self-interested governments, by those charged with holding these governments to account, and perhaps by our own disinterest in and complacency about the state of our politics, culture and society. This book was written in response to this situation, as an attempt to better understand it and point to some of the ways in which Australia might move closer to what it should be.

With the various lockdowns, border closures and other forms of isolation that prevailed over the periods in which I compiled this book, there are fewer people than usual to thank for assistance and support. It was very much a lone project, knocked up in my study looking out over the hills in the Byron hinterland. I do have some folks whose assistance I would like to acknowledge, however. The anonymous readers of the original proposal made some very helpful suggestions which have been incorporated into the book. Comments from colleagues Chris Healy, Rod Tiffen, Kate Darian-Smith and Jim McKay were appreciated, as was the support from Lucy Russell and Christine Turner. Editorial input from Madonna Duffy and Jacqueline Blanchard at UQP and from my editor Julian Welch has been substantial and I am grateful for their contribution to making this a better book.

Federal, New South Wales
June 2023

Notes

Introduction: 'It just feels like Australia has shrunk'

1   See Laura Tingle, 'Political amnesia: How we forgot how to govern', *Quarterly Essay*, 60, Black Inc., Melbourne, 2015, pp. 1–86.

2   Peter Lewis, 'Distrusting the information we receive, too many of us are carrying on business as usual', *The Guardian*, 24 March 2020; Mark Evans, 'Scott Morrison's pandemic popularity boost has vanished, along with public trust in our politicians', *The Guardian*, 16 November 2021.

3   George Megalogenis, *Balancing act: Australia between recession and renewal*, Black Inc., Melbourne, 2017; Bernard Keane, *The mess we're in: How our politics went to hell and dragged us with it*, Allen & Unwin, Sydney, 2018; Laura Tingle, 'Follow the leader: Democracy and the rise of the strongman', *Quarterly Essay*, 71, Black Inc., Melbourne, 2018, pp. 1–90; Niki Savva, 'Damaged not destroyed: PM in trouble but could again land on his feet', *The Sydney Morning Herald*, 5 August 2021.

4   Gabrielle Chan, *Rusted off: Why country Australia is fed up*, Vintage, Sydney, 2018; Keane, *The mess we're in*; Richard Denniss, *Dead right: How neoliberalism ate itself and what comes next*, Black Inc., Melbourne, 2019; Keith Dowding, *It's the government, stupid: How governments blame citizens for their own policies*, Bristol University Press, Bristol, 2020; Sean Kelly, 'Morrison's new tactic? A pledge to return things to the way they were', *The Sydney Morning Herald*, 15 November 2021.

5   Greg Noble, 'Cosmopolitan habits: The capacities and habitats of intercultural conviviality', *Body and Society*, vol. 19, nos. 2–3, 2013, pp. 162–85. It should be noted here that 'hyperdiversity', in this context, is seen as something of a challenge to be managed by those in the

community accustomed to a more traditionally monocultural society and confronted by the cultural transformation of, for instance, their local shopping street.

6   Richard Florida, *The rise of the creative class*, Basic Books, London, 2002.
7   Denniss, *Dead right*.
8   John Ellis, *Seeing things: Television in an age of uncertainty*, I.B. Taurus, London, 2002.

Chapter 1. Diminished leaders, bad politics

1   Martin McKenzie-Murray, 'The little premier that might have', *The Monthly*, 8 October 2021.
2   This includes conservative political journalists such as Niki Savva, Chris Uhlmann and Peter van Onselen; centre-left commentators such as George Megalogenis, Bernard Keane and Laura Tingle; political scientists such as Keith Dowding and Richard Denniss; public pollsters such as Peter Lewis; economics correspondents such as Ross Gittins and Shane Wright; and a raft of former politicians, including Labor's Barry Jones, Lindsay Tanner and Kevin Rudd, and former Coalition leaders John Hewson and Malcolm Turnbull.
3   Judith Brett, *Doing politics: Writing on public life*, Text, Melbourne, 2021, p. 4.
4   Tim Dunlop, 'Tony Abbott and the normalisation of bad politics', ABC News, 23 April 2015; Ross Gittins, 'Sometime, somewhere we will find leaders interested in doing a better job', *The Sydney Morning Herald*, 16 July 2021.
5   Brett, *Doing politics*, p. 1.
6   Lindsay Tanner, *Sideshow: Dumbing down democracy*, Scribe, Melbourne, 2011, p. 8.
7   Keane, *The mess we're in*, p. 137.
8   Anne Davies, 'Party hardly: Why Australia's big political parties are struggling to compete with grassroots campaigns', *The Guardian*, 13 December 2020.
9   Lewis, 'Distrusting the information we receive ...'.
10 Amanda Roe, 'Television satire, democracy and the decay of public language: John Clarke's verbal caricature', *Media International Australia*, vol. 121, no. 1, pp. 93–104.
11 Jess Davis and Nathan Morris, 'Growing dissatisfaction with federal politics sees Coalition seats under threat from independents', ABC News, 15 September 2021; Peter Hartcher, 'Morrison may lie, but his real test is not honesty – it's about trust', *The Sydney Morning Herald*, 20 November 2021; Jacqueline Maley, '"The real reason is the environment": Allegra Spender to run as Wentworth independent', *The Sydney Morning Herald*, 19 November 2021; Katharine Murphy, 'Former Liberal leader to join

forces with Labor veteran in bid to target Morrison ahead of election',
The Guardian, 19 November 2021; Niki Savva, 'Fresh voices rise in
Liberal heartland', *The Sydney Morning Herald*, 16 September 2021.

12 Murphy, 'Former Liberal leader to join forces with Labor veteran …'.
13 David Crowe and Shane Wright, 'Former judge labels $660 million car
park fund 'corruption', *The Sydney Morning Herald*, 22 July 2021.
14 Rodney Tiffen, *Disposable leaders: Media and leadership coups from Menzies
to Abbott*, NewSouth, Sydney, 2017, p. 2.
15 Ibid., p. 227.
16 Nick Bryant, *The rise and fall of Australia: How a great nation lost its way*,
Bantam, Sydney, 2014, p. 15.
17 These accounts of the disposable leaders are necessarily brief here; a
more detailed and analytical account of Rudd, Gillard and Abbott can
be found in Tiffen (2017). Aaron Patrick (2013) presents an account of
the downfall of the Rudd/Gillard government, while Niki Savva (2016;
2019; 2022) chronicles the destruction of the Abbott government, the
fall of Malcolm Turnbull and the unravelling of Scott Morrison.
18 Tiffen, *Disposable leaders*, p. 19.
19 Kate Ellis, *Sex, lies and question time: Why the successes and struggles of
women in Australia's parliament matters to us all*, Hardie Grant, Melbourne,
2021; Julia Gillard (ed.), *Not now, not ever: Ten years on from the misogyny
speech*, Vintage Books, Melbourne, 2022.
20 Dunlop, 'Tony Abbott and the normalisation of bad politics'.
21 Tingle, 'Follow the leader', p. 81.
22 Savva, 'Damaged not destroyed …'.
23 Sarah Martin, 'The Delta variant has shown Fortress Australia to be a
house of cards due to the Coalition's vaccine stroll-out', *The Guardian*, 17
July 2021.
24 Savva ended up describing Morrison as the 'worst prime minister' she
has covered as a journalist (Niki Savva, *Bulldozed: Scott Morrison's fall and
Anthony Albanese's rise*, Scribe, Melbourne, 2022, p. 387).
25 Maley, '"The real reason is the environment" …'.
26 Chan, *Rusted off*, p. 14.
27 Tom Nichols, *The death of expertise: The campaign against established
knowledge and why it matters*, Oxford University Press, New York, 2017,
p. x.
28 This argument was well made by Laura Tingle in 'Follow the leader'.
29 David Marr and Marian Wilkinson, *Dark victory: How a government
lied its way to political triumph*, Allen & Unwin, Sydney, 2003; George
Megalogenis, *Faultlines: Race, work, and the politics of changing Australia*,
Scribe, Melbourne, 2003; Dunlop, 'Tony Abbott and the normalisation
of bad politics'.
30 Lewis, 'Distrusting the information we receive …'.

31 Sarah Martin, 'Scott Morrison takes misinformation mainstream and dares Labor to offer more than nothing', *The Guardian*, 13 November 2021.

32 Warwick Smith, 'Chalmers hasn't delivered a wellbeing budget, but it's a step in the right direction', *The Conversation*, 26 October 2022.

Chapter 2. How good's the status quo?

1 David Taylor, 'Rich getting richer and poor slipping further back, with youth inequality growing fastest, ACOSS says', ABC News, 2 September 2020.

2 Brendan Coates and Carmela Chivers, 'Rising inequality isn't about incomes: it's almost all about housing', *The Conversation*, 19 September 2019.

3 Ibid.

4 Keane, *The mess we're in*, p. 27.

5 Ken Hillis, Michael Petit and Kylie Jarrett, *Google and the culture of search*, Routledge, London and New York, 2013; Mark Andrejevic, *Infoglut: How too much information is changing the way we think and know*, Routledge, New York and London, 2013; Anna Cristina Pertierra and Graeme Turner, 'Cultural participation and belonging', in Tony Bennett, David Carter, Modesto Gayo, Michelle Kelly and Greg Noble (eds), *Fields, capitals, habitus: Australian culture, inequalities and social divisions*, Routledge, London and New York, 2021, pp. 280–93.

6 Sean Kelly, 'Morrison's new tactic?', *The Sydney Morning Herald*, 15 November 2021.

7 Gittins, 'Sometime, somewhere we will find leaders …'.

8 Amy Remeikis, 'Scott Morrison's "can-do capitalism" is a hypocritical example of a "do nothing" leadership', *The Guardian*, 17 November 2021; Niki Savva, 'PM employs risky strategy to win the votes of disaffected Australians', *The Sydney Morning Herald*, 18 November 2021.

9 Kelly, 'Morrison's new tactic …'.

10 Denniss, *Dead right*, p. 134.

11 National Museum of Australia, *Glorious days: Social laboratory*, 2022, https://www.nma.gov.au/exhibitions/glorious-days-social-laboratory.

12 George Megalogenis, *Australia's second chance: What our history tells us about our future*, Hamish Hamilton, Sydney, 2015, pp. 86–87.

13 Anthony Moran, *Australia: Nation, belonging, and globalization*, Routledge, New York and London, 2005, pp. 23, 26.

14 Bryant, *The rise and fall of Australia*, p. 15.

15 Megalogenis, *Australia's second chance*, p. 284.

16 Bryant, *The rise and fall of Australia*, p. 15.

17 Denniss, *Dead right*, p. 4.

18 Keane, *The mess we're in*, p. 39.

19 Dowding, *It's the government, stupid*, p. 4.

20 Tingle, 'Follow the leader', p. 22.

21 Wayne Errington and Peter van Onselen, *How good is Scott Morrison?*, Hachette, Sydney, 2021.

22 David Crowe and Shane Wright, 'Former judge labels $660 million car park fund "corruption"', *The Sydney Morning Herald*, 22 July 2021.

23 Marian Wilkinson, *The carbon club: How a network of influential climate sceptics, politicians and business leaders fought to control Australia's climate policy*, Allen & Unwin, Sydney, 2020; George Megalogenis, 'Exit strategy: Politics after the pandemic', *Quarterly Essay*, 82, Black Inc., Melbourne, 2021.

24 Errington and Van Onselen, *How good is Scott Morrison?*, pp. 187, 181.

25 Gittins, 'Sometime, somewhere we will find leaders …'.

26 David McKnight, *Populism now! The case for progressive populism*, NewSouth, Sydney, 2018, p. 64.

27 Chris Wallace, 'Albanese goes back to the future for governing', *The Sydney Morning Herald*, 21 July 2022.

28 Megalogenis, *Australia's second chance*; Megalogenis, 'Exit strategy'; Tingle, 'Follow the leader'; John Quiggin, 'Dismembering government: New public management and why the Commonwealth government can't do anything anymore', *The Monthly*, September 2021; Dowding, *It's the government, stupid*.

29 Tiffen, *Disposable leaders*, p. 234.

30 Wallace, 'Albanese goes back to the future …'.

31 John Daley, *Gridlock: Removing barriers to policy reform*, Grattan Institute, Melbourne, 2021, p. 47.

32 I am speaking here from experience, having served on many federal committees and working groups dealing with research, higher education policy and the national curriculum over the period 2004–2018.

33 Daley, *Gridlock*, p. 19.

34 Ibid., p. 47.

35 Ibid., p. 48.

36 Julianne Schultz, 'How Morrison killed the public service', *The Saturday Paper*, 12–18 February 2022.

37 Graeme Turner, *Ending the affair: The decline of television current affairs in Australia*, UNSW Press, Sydney, 2005.

38 I acknowledge that not everybody agrees with this analysis; see also Brian McNair, Terry Flew, Stephen Harrington and Adam Swift, *Politics, media and democracy in Australia: Public and producer perceptions of the political public sphere*, Routledge, London, 2017.

39 Tiffen, *Disposable leaders*, p. 237.

40 Brett, *Doing politics*, p. 4.

41 David Crowe, '"Ministers have too much control": $10b in taxpayer funds put at risk', *The Sydney Morning Herald*, 3 August 2021.

42   Ibid.

43   Crowe and Wright, 'Former judge labels $660 million car park fund "corruption"'.

44   Lewis, 'Distrusting the information we receive…'.

45   Evans, 'Scott Morrison's pandemic popularity …', *The Guardian*, 16 November 2021.

46   Ibid.

47   Steven Levitsky and Daniel Ziblatt, *How democracies die: What history reveals about our future*, Viking, New York, 2018, pp. 7–8.

48   Andrew Leigh, 'Charities are sick of fighting off attacks by the Morrison government', *The Guardian*, 15 January 2022.

49   Richard Denniss, *Big: The role of the state in the modern economy*, Monash University Publishing, Melbourne, 2022, p. 32; Brian Toohey, 'The rise and rise of Australian authoritarianism', *The Saturday Paper*, 17–23 July 2021; Peter Greste, *The first casualty: From the front lines of the global war on journalism*, Viking, Melbourne, 2017.

50   Levitsky and Ziblatt, *How democracies die*, chapter 5.

51   Crowe and Wright, 'Former judge labels $660 milliom car park fund "corruption"'.

52   Brett, *Doing politics*, p. 5.

53   Katharine Murphy, 'Lone wolf: Albanese and the new politics', *Quarterly Essay*, 88, Black Inc., Melbourne, 2022.

Chapter 3. Down in the hole: The consequences of neoliberalism

1   Paul Karp, 'Australia's living standards have risen and economy is roaring back, Deloitte says', *The Guardian*, 12 April 2021.

2   Michael Pusey, *Economic rationalism in Canberra: A nation building state changes its mind*, Cambridge University Press, Melbourne, 1991.

3   I realise that this is a term that has been much debated, and its meanings and provenance much contested in the academic arena. Here, I am choosing not to get entangled in these debates, and I deploy the term in ways that are consistent with its common usage in public commentary.

4   Michael Pusey, *The experience of middle Australia: The dark side of economic reform*, Cambridge University Press, Melbourne, 2003.

5   Denniss, *Big*, p. 2.

6   Megalogenis, 'Exit strategy', p. 7.

7   McKnight, *Populism now!*, p. 66.

8   Denniss, *Dead right*, p. 2.

9   Ibid.

10   Megalogenis, 'Exit strategy', p. 11.

11   Paul Collier and John Kay, *Greed is dead: Politics after individualism*, Allen Lane, London, 2020, p. 22.

12   Ibid.

13   Keane, *The mess we're in*, p. 151.
14   Evan Osnos, *Wildland: The making of America's fury*, Bloomsbury, New York, 2021, p. 168.
15   This is an important point to acknowledge: many were much better citizens than that. See Collier and Kay, *Greed is dead*, p. 21.
16   Ibid. p. 1.
17   John Hewson, 'The merit of privatisation has been lost through greed', *The Saturday Paper*, 4–10 September 2021.
18   Thomas Piketty (translated by Arthur Goldhammer), *Capital in the twenty-first century*, Belknap Press of Harvard University Press, Cambridge MA, 2014, pp.537, 1.
19   Dowding, *It's the government, stupid*, pp. 7, xii.
20   Brett, *Doing politics*, p. 10.
21   Dowding, *It's the government, stupid*, p. 14.
22   Ibid., p. 7.
23   Stephanie Kelton, *The deficit myth: Modern monetary theory and how to build a better economy*, John Murray, London, 2020, p. 2.
24   McKnight, *Populism now!*, pp. 5–6.
25   Ibid., p. 6.
26   Ibid., p. 166.
27   Deborah Warr, Keith Jacobs and Henry Paternoster, 'Bogan talk: What it says (and can't say) about class in Australia', in Steven Threadgold and Jessica Gerrard (eds), *Class in Australia*, Monash University Publishing, Melbourne, 2022, pp. 128–29.
28   Jessica Gerrard and Steven Threadgold, 'Class in Australia: Public debates and research directions in a settler colony', in Threadgold and Gerrard (eds), *Class in Australia*, pp. 4–5.
29   UNSW Media, 'Reducing poverty and inequality in Australia is possible, report says', UNSW Sydney Newsroom, 2 March 2022, https://newsroom.unsw.edu.au/news/social-affairs/reducing-poverty-and-inequality-australia-possible-report-says.
30   Coates and Chivers, 'Rising inequality …'.
31   Keane, *The mess we're in*, p. 28.
32   Ibid., p. 29.
33   Denniss, *Dead right*, pp. 59, 61, 5, 11.
34   For examples of this, see the extended debate that followed the publication of Denniss's *Quarterly Essay* (no. 71, 2018), which formed the basis for the book-length version of *Dead right*.
35   Michael Lewis, *The fifth risk: Undoing democracy*, Norton, New York, 2018.
36   Denniss, *Big*, p. 7.
37   Judith Brett, 'COVID exposed our fractured national identity, but state-based loyalties were rising long before', *The Conversation*, 20 October 2021.
38   Moran, *Australia*, p. 30.

39 Andrew Taylor, "Pure greed": Government task force criticised as regional Australia revolts over bank closures', *The Sydney Morning Herald*, 30 January 2022.

40 Moran, *Australia*, p. 31.

41 Quiggin, 'Dismembering government', p. 6.

42 Nicholas Reece, 'Failure of the federation has gone too far this time', *The Sydney Morning Herald*, 9 January 2022; Schultz, 'How Morrison killed the public service'.

43 Pusey, *Economic rationalism in Canberra*.

44 Quiggin, 'Dismembering government', p. 2.

45 Ibid., p. 3.

46 Reece, 'Failure of the federation …'.

47 Quiggin, 'Dismembering government', p. 4.

48 Denniss, *Big*, p. 61.

49 See David Rowe, Graeme Turner and Emma Waterton, 'Introduction: Making culture', in David Rowe, Graeme Turner and Emma Waterton (eds), *Making culture: Commercialisation, transnationalism, and the state of 'nationing' in contemporary Australia*, Routledge, London and New York, 2018, pp. 1–12.

50 Graeme Turner, *Making it national: Nationalism and Australian popular culture*, Allen & Unwin, Sydney, 1994.

51 Ibid., p. 29.

52 Ibid., p. 16.

53 Ibid.

54 As I pointed out, this is not at all a 'natural' connection: there are many alternative ways of conceiving the state of the nation, 'most of which would relegate "the economy" to a secondary role' (*Making it national*, p. 16).

55 Ibid., p. 17.

56 Ibid.

57 Ibid.

58 Michael Emmison, '"The economy": Its emergence in popular discourse', in Howard Davis and Paul Walton (eds), *Language, image, media*, Basil Blackwell, London, 1983, pp. 154, 152.

59 Turner, *Making it national*, p. 40.

Chapter 4. Media and information 2.0: What we know now, and how we know it

1 Andrejevic, *Infoglut*, p. 2.

2 Jonathan Cohn, *The burden of choice: Recommendations, subversion, and algorithmic culture*, Rutgers University Press, New Brunswick, 2019.

3 Victor Pickard, *Democracy without journalism? Confronting the misinformation society*, Oxford University Press, New York, 2020.

4   Mark Andrejevic, *Automated media*, Routledge, New York and London, 2019, p. 56.
5   Jim McGuigan, *Cool capitalism*, Pluto, London, 2009.
6   Howard Rheingold, *The virtual community: Homesteading on the electronic frontier* (revised edition), MIT Press, Cambridge MA, 2000.
7   Shoshana Zuboff, *The age of surveillance capitalism: The fight for a human future at the new frontier of power*, Public Affairs, New York, 2019, p. 9.
8   Graeme Turner, *Re-inventing the media*, Routledge, London and New York, 2016, p. 39; Graeme Turner, Frances Bonner and P. David Marshall, *Fame games: The production of celebrity in Australia*, Cambridge University Press, Melbourne, 2000; Nick Couldry, *Media, society, world: Social theory and digital media practice*, Polity, Cambridge, 2012, pp. 19–20.
9   Turner, *Re-inventing the media*, p. 51.
10 Taina Bucher, *Facebook*, Polity, Cambridge, 2022.
11 Osnos, *Wildland*, pp. 308–09.
12 Ed Coper, *Facts and other lies: Welcome to the disinformation age*, Allen & Unwin, Sydney, 2022, p. 344.
13 Zuboff, *The age of surveillance capitalism*, pp. 85–95.
14 Coper, *Facts and other lies*, p. 153.
15 Bucher, *Facebook*, p. 117.
16 José van Dijck, Thomas Poell and Martijn de Waal, *The platform society: Public values in a connected world*, Oxford University Press, New York, 2018.
17 'Dark' ads are targeted to specific online users who meet particular demographic parameters picked up by data mining. The ads might appear only to these individuals; even those individuals do not know who else is receiving the ads. Dark ads fall outside the vision of regulatory authorities, and raise significant issues of transparency, accountability and social cohesion. See Verity Trott, Nina Li, Robbie Fordyce and Mark Andrejevic, 'Shedding light on "dark" ads', *Continuum*, vol. 35, no. 5, 2021, p. 762.
18 Bucher, *Facebook*, p. 193.
19 Ibid., p. 4.
20 Ibid., p. 198.
21 Recent examples of this 'techlash' include Taplin's *Move fast and break things* (2017), Wachter-Boettcher's *Technically wrong* (2017), Arai's *The hype machine* (2020) and Frenkel and King's *An ugly truth* (2021).
22 Zuboff, *The age of surveillance capitalism*, p. 10.
23 Graeme Turner, *Ordinary people and the media: The demotic turn*, Sage, London, 2010.
24 Stuart Cunningham and David Craig, *Social media entertainment: The new intersection of Hollywood and Silicon Valley*, New York University Press, New York, 2019.
25 McNair et al., *Politics, media and democracy in Australia*.

26 Cass Sunstein, *Republic.com 2.0*, Princeton University Press, Princeton, 2009.

27 Eli Pariser, *The filter bubble: What the internet is hiding from you*, Penguin, New York, 2011.

28 Andrejevic, *Automated media*, p. 48.

29 Ibid.

30 Ibid., p. 47.

31 Ibid., p. 48.

32 Ibid., p. 49.

33 Ibid., p. 52.

34 Ibid., p. 60.

35 Cohn, *The burden of choice*, p. 36.

36 Sarah Banet-Weiser, *Authentic: The politics of ambivalence in a brand culture*, New York University Press, New York and London, 2012.

37 Taina Bucher, *If … then: Algorithmic power and politics*, Oxford University Press, New York, 2018.

38 Andrejevic, *Automated media*, p. 29.

39 Cohn, *The burden of choice*; Kate Crawford, *Atlas of AI: Power, politics and the planetary costs of artificial intelligence*, Yale University Press, New Haven, 2021; Virginia Eubanks, *Automating inequality: How high-tech tools profile, police, and punish the poor*, St Martin's Press, New York, 2018.

40 Cohn, *The burden of choice*, p. 12.

41 Eubanks, *Automating inequality*, p. 3.

42 Ibid., p. 12.

43 Luke Henriques-Gomes, 'Robodebt scandal: More than 3,000 deceased estates owed refunds by Australian government', *The Guardian*, 30 October 2020; Caroline Schelle, '"Shameful" robodebt chapter ends with $1.7bn settlement', News.com.au, 11 June 2021; Peter Whiteford, 'Robodebt was a fiasco with a cost we have yet to fully appreciate', *The Conversation*, 16 November 2020.

44 Coper, *Facts and other lies*, p. 62.

45 At the time of writing, former prime ministers Rudd and Turnbull are fronting a campaign to establish a royal commission into the dominance and behaviour of the Murdoch press.

46 Coper, *Facts and other lies*, p. 62.

47 Matthew Ricketson and Patrick Mullins, *Who needs the ABC? Why taking it for granted is no longer an option*, Scribe, Melbourne, 2022, p. 17.

48 Turner, *Ending the affair*.

49 Deloitte Touche Tohmatsu, *Media consumer survey 2021: Australian digital entertainment audience preferences* (tenth edition), Deloitte, 2021.

50 That said, the report found that there is a shared concern (64 per cent) across all these demographics about the amount of 'fake news' in their newsfeeds online.

51 Coper, *Facts and other lies*, p. 164.
52 Ibid., p. 98.
53 Piketty, *Capital in the twenty-first century*, p. 21.
54 Nichols, *The death of expertise*, p. xix.
55 Ibid., p. xx.
56 Ibid.
57 Ibid., pp. xxi–xxii.
58 Ibid., p. 211.
59 Marc Hudson, 'Tony Abbott, once the "climate weathervane", has long since rusted stuck', *The Conversation*, 9 October 2017.
60 Nick O'Malley and Laura Chung, 'The failures that left Australians facing floods alone began years ago', *The Sydney Morning Herald*, 19 March 2022.
61 Disclosure: I served two terms on PMSEIC during the Rudd/Gillard/Rudd administrations.
62 Amanda Meade, 'ABC's Norman Swan denies "rancour" with chief medical officer after PM's office intervention on coronavirus', *The Guardian*, 25 March 2020.
63 Errington and Van Onselen, *How good is Scott Morrison?*, pp. 116–17.
64 Evans, 'Scott Morrison's pandemic popularity …'.
65 Errington and Van Onselen, *How good is Scott Morrison?*, p. 117.
66 Ibid.
67 Stephen Matchett, 'PM explains: There are unis and there are unis', *Campus Morning Mail*, 15 March 2022.
68 Errington and Van Onselen, *How good is Scott Morrison?*, p. 117.
69 Alliance for Journalists' Freedom, *Press freedom in Australia: With light, trust*, White Paper, May 2019.
70 Max Walden, 'Australia lags behind New Zealand, Taiwan and Timor-Leste on World Press Freedom Index', ABC News, 4 May 2022.
71 Toohey, 'The rise and rise of Australian authoritarianism'.

Chapter 5. What's become of the public good?

1 Stefan Collini, *What are universities for?*, Penguin, London, 2012, p. 110.
2 Brett Hutchins, '"Crossing the technical Rubicon": Marketizing culture and fields of the digital', in Rowe, Turner and Waterton (eds), *Making culture*, p. 106.
3 Ibid., p. 108.
4 Moran, *Australia*, pp. 25–26.
5 Rowe, Turner and Waterton, 'Introduction'.
6 Errington and Van Onselen, *How good is Scott Morrison?*, pp. 185, 187, 188.
7 Ross Gittins, 'It hasn't taken Scott Morrison long to start playing friends and enemies', *The Sydney Morning Herald*, 24 June 2020; Mike Seccombe, 'The plot to destroy the Human Rights Commission', *The Saturday*

Paper, 16–22 April 2022; Michael Ward, Alexandra Wake, Matthew Ricketson and Patrick Mullins, 'No-one is talking about ABC funding in this election campaign. Here's why they should be', *The Conversation*, 28 April 2022; Leigh, 'Charities are sick ...'; Kristine Ziwica, 'New front in Coalition war on charities', *The Saturday Paper*, 14–20 May 2022.

8   Collini, *What are universities for?*, p. 97.

9   Robert Reich, *The common good*, Vintage, New York, 2018, p. 36.

10   Reich, *The common good*.

11   Van Dijck, Poell and De Waal, *The platform society*, p. 22.

12   Collini, What are universities for?, p. 94.

13   John Fiske, Power plays power works, Verso, London, 1993, p. 29.

14   What follows is necessarily a very brief discussion of the ABC's place in the nation, and its relation to government, but there is a 2022 book which lays out a fuller history: Matthew Ricketson and Patrick Mullins, *Who needs the ABC?*.

15   Ricketson and Mullins, *Who needs the ABC?*, pp. 27–54.

16   Disclosure: I conducted a research project for the ABC as part of the organisation's response to this review, comparing its news coverage with that of the commercial networks.

17   Karl Quinn, 'Biased against the left or right? The social media onslaught targeting the ABC', *The Sydney Morning Herald*, 1 May 2022.

18   Jennifer Duke, 'Was the ABC's funding cut?', *The Sydney Morning Herald*, 17 August 2020.

19   Ward, Wake, Ricketson and Mullins, 'No-one is talking about ABC funding ...'. They construct this figure from a range of budgetary measures over the last eight years – that is, since the election of the Abbott government. These include the axeing of the Australia Network ($186 million), the 2014 cut of 1 per cent to the ABC's operating budget ($72 million), and the 'efficiency' savings of $353 million. Finally, there is the addition of the 2017 cut to tied funding initiatives ($122 million) and the 2018 freeze on indexation ($84 million). A full record of this research appears in the appendices to Ricketson and Mullins, *Who needs the ABC?*.

20   Errington and Van Onselen, How good is Scott Morrison?, p. 193; Australia Institute, 'No more ABC cuts welcome, however, time to restore funding', 7 February 2022; Duke, 'Was the ABC's funding cut?'.

21   Ward, Wake, Ricketson and Mullins, 'No-one is talking about ABC funding ...'. Ward, Wake, Ricketson and Mullins, 'No-one is talking about ABC funding ...'.

22   Turner, Ending the affair, p. 37. In a revealing comparison to the present situation, my research into *This Day Tonight* found that its audience 'seems to have regarded the controversial nature of the program and its propensity for offending politicians and other members of the establishment as among its most attractive characteristics' (p. 36).

23 Ricketson and Mullins, *Who needs the ABC?*, p. 3.
24 Ken Inglis, *Whose ABC? The Australian Broadcasting Corporation 1983–2006*, Black Inc., Melbourne, 2006, pp. 188–90.
25 Kevin Rudd, 'Far from having a leftwing bias, the ABC has been tamed by cuts and incessant attacks', *The Guardian*, 10 May 2022.
26 Ricketson and Mullins, *Who needs the ABC?*, p. 3.
27 Rick Morton, 'The vote: Why you won't see a debate on the ABC', *The Saturday Paper*, 10 May 2022.
28 McKenzie Wark, *The virtual republic: Australia's culture wars of the 1990s*, Allen & Unwin, Sydney, 1997.
29 Ricketson and Mullins, *Who needs the ABC?*, p. 175.
30 Anne Davies, 'John Howard and the ABC: Desire for cuts came up against liberal support for the broadcaster', *The Guardian*, 1 January 2022.
31 Rudd, 'Far from having a leftwing bias …'.
32 Alison Croggon, 'The campaign to destroy the arts', *The Saturday Paper*, 16–22 April 2022.
33 Ibid.
34 Elissa Blake, 'Australia's arts sector shredded by latest Covid shutdown and won't survive without government help, report warns', *The Guardian*, 26 July 2021.
35 Ibid.
36 Alison Pennington and Ben Eltham, *Creativity in crisis: Rebooting Australia's arts and entertainment sector after Covid*, Centre for Future Work, July 2021.
37 Croggon, 'The campaign to destroy the arts …'.
38 Errington and Van Onselen, *How good is Scott Morrison?*, p. 198.
39 Blake, 'Australia's arts sector shredded …'.
40 J.L. Trembath and K. Fielding, *Australia's cultural and creative economy: A 21st century guide*, A New Approach, Australian Academy of the Humanities, Canberra, 2020, pp. 11–12.
41 Croggon, 'The campaign to destroy the arts …'.
42 Mark Banks and Justin O'Connor, '"A plague upon your howling": Art and culture in the viral emergency', *Cultural Trends*, vol. 30, no. 1, 2021, p. 5.
43 Seccombe, 'The plot to destroy the Human Rights Commission'.
44 Emma Waterton, 'A history of heritage policy in Australia: From hope to philanthropy', in Rowe, Turner and Waterton (eds), *Making culture*, pp. 75–86.
45 Commonwealth of Australia, *Creative nation: Commonwealth cultural policy* (revised edition), Department of Communications and the Arts, Canberra, 1994; Commonwealth of Australia, *Creative Australia: National cultural policy*, Australian Government, Canberra, 2013; Rowe, Turner and Waterton, 'Introduction', p. 9.
46 Bennett, Carter, Gayo, Kelly and Noble (eds), *Fields, capitals, habitus*, p. 4.
47 Megalogenis, 'Exit strategy', p. 52.

48 Estimates range between 20,000 and 40,000 jobs lost. It is instructive to place these figures of actual job losses in one year, effectively seen as acceptable by the government of the day, against decades of resistance to risking any of the 38,000 mining jobs that might be lost over the next decade if fossil fuels are phased out.

49 Frank Larkins, 'Australian university staff job losses exceed pandemic financial outcomes', Melbourne CSHE, 9 May 2022.

50 Stephen Knight, *The university is closed for open day: Themes and scenes from 21st century Australia*, Melbourne University Press, Melbourne, 2019, p. 217.

51 Gittins, 'It hasn't taken Scott Morrison long …'.

52 Megalogenis, 'Exit strategy', p. 55.

53 Brett, *Doing politics*, p. 6.

54 Megalogenis, 'Exit strategy', pp. 51–52.

55 Ibid., p. 61.

56 I was directly involved in negotiations and working groups with government over higher education research policy over this period, dealing with ministers from both the Coalition and Labor, mostly as a representative of the Australian Academy of the Humanities. Ministers Nelson and Bishop were both diligent and accessible ministers, while Kim Carr was a vigorous advocate for the sector, and for the humanities. When Abbott was elected, however, access to the minister was shut down and the new regime of adversarial relationship with the universities, and with academic expertise, began.

57 Collini, *What are universities for?*, p. 91.

58 Megalogenis, 'Exit strategy', p. 58.

59 Ian Marshman and Frank Larkins, 'The vocationalisation of university education', *Campus Morning Mail*, 21 June 2020.

60 Rick Morton, 'The "institutional rot" of Australian universities', *The Saturday Paper*, 4–10 June 2022.

61 Elizabeth Farrelly, 'The decline of universities, where students are customers and academics itinerant workers', *The Sydney Morning Herald*, 30 May 2020.

62 Collini, *What are universities for?*, p. 91.

63 Stuart Macintyre, André Brett and Gwilym Croucher, *No end of a lesson: Australia's unified system of higher education*, Melbourne University Press, Melbourne, 2017, pp. 246–47.

64 Ibid., p. 247.

65 Hazel Ferguson, *A guide to Australian government funding for higher education learning and teaching*, Research Papers, Parliamentary Library, Department of Parliamentary Services, Parliament of Australia, 23 April 2021.

66 Tony Coady (ed.), *Why universities matter: A conversation about values, means and directions*, Allen & Unwin, Sydney, 2000; Simon Marginson

and Mark Considine, *The enterprise university: Power, governance and reinvention in Australia*, Cambridge University Press, Cambridge, 2000; Peter Coaldrake and Lawrence Stedman, *Raising the stakes: Gambling with the future of universities*, University of Queensland Press, St Lucia, 2013; Hannah Forsyth, *A history of the modern Australian university*, NewSouth, Sydney, 2014.

67 James Guthrie, 'A summit to solve Australia's university crisis', *Campus Morning Mail*, 15 May 2022.
68 Reich, *The common good*, pp. 93–94.
69 Keane, *The mess we're in*, p. 157.
70 Knight, *The university is closed for open day*, pp. 210–11.

Chapter 6. What's to be done?

1 Benedict Anderson, *Imagined communities: Reflections on the origin and spread of nationalism*, Verso, London, 1983, p. 15.
2 Nadia Kaneva (ed.), *Branding post-communist nations: Marketizing national identities in the 'new' Europe*, Routledge, New York, 2012.
3 The work of Zala Volcic and Mark Andrejevic, in particular, has focused on the process of inventing national identities within the complex ethno-political environment of the nation-states emerging from the former Yugoslavia, in which the establishment of a national identity has been an urgent political objective. See Zala Volcic and Mark Andrejevic (eds), *Commercial nationalism: Selling the nation and nationalizing the sell*, Palgrave Macmillan, London, 2016.
4 Craig Calhoun, *Nations matter: Culture, history, and the cosmopolitan dream*, Routledge, London and New York, 2007; Terry Flew, Petros Iosifidis and Jeanette Steemers (eds), *Global media and national policies: The return of the state*, Palgrave Macmillan, London, 2016.
5 Flew, Iosifidis and Steemers (eds), *Global media and national policies*.
6 Anderson, *Imagined communities*.
7 Andreas Hepp, *Cultures of mediatization*, Polity, London, 2013.
8 Kieran Pender, 'No relief', *The Monthly*, 6 April 2022.
9 Heath Gilmore, 'Mick Fanning, the group text and the mud army fighting for the Northern Rivers', *The Sydney Morning Herald*, 9 March 2022.
10 I live in the Northern Rivers, so I have been seeing this unfold, day after day, in my own community and in those nearby.
11 Daniel Dayan, 'Sharing and showing: Television as monstration', *Annals of the American Academy of Political and Social Science*, vol. 625, 2009, pp. 19–31.
12 Pertierra and Turner, *Locating television*, p. 77.
13 Ibid., p. 61.
14 Graeme Turner, 'Ethics, entertainment and the tabloid: The case of talkback radio in Australia', in Catharine Lumby and Elspeth Probyn

(eds), *Remote control: New media, new ethics*, Cambridge University Press, Melbourne, 2003, pp. 87–99.

15   Graeme Turner, 'Some things we should know about talkback radio', *Media International Australia*, vol. 122, February 2007, pp. 73–80.

16   Pertierra and Turner, *Locating television*, p. 62.

17   Bronwyn Carlson and Jeff Berglund (eds), *Indigenous peoples rise up: The global ascendency of social media activism*, Rutgers University Press, New Brunswick, 2021.

18   George Yúdice, 'Community', in Tony Bennett, Lawrence Grossberg and Meaghan Morris (eds), *New keywords: A revised vocabulary of culture and society*, Blackwell, Malden MA, 2001, pp. 51–53.

19   Pertierra and Turner, *Locating television*, pp. 80–81.

20   Ibid., p. 81. A full discussion of the relationship between television, new media and community can be found in Chapter 3 of *Locating television*.

21   Andrejevic, *Automated media*, p. 57.

22   Jonathan Taplin, Move fast and break things: How Facebook, Google and Amazon have cornered culture and undermined democracy, Pan Macmillan, London, 2017; Zuboff, *The age of surveillance capitalism*; Sheera Frenkel and Cecilia Kang, *An ugly truth: Inside Face██ ▓▓ battle for domination*, Harper, New York, 2021.

23   Brett, 'COVID exposed our fractured national identity▓▓

24   Pertierra and Turner, 'Cultural participation and belon███▓, p. 291.

25   Damien Cave, *Into the rip: How the Australian way of ris▓ made my family, stronger, happier … and less American*, Scribner, Sydney, 2021.

26   Sabina Mihelj, *Media nations: Communicating belonging and exclusion in the modern world*, Palgrave Macmillan, London, 2011, p. 1.

27   Calhoun, *Nations matter*, p. 1.

28   Stuart Macintyre and Anna Clark, *The history wars*, Melbourne University Press, Melbourne, 2003.

29   Brett, *Doing politics*, pp. 155–67.

30   Wark, *The virtual republic*.

31   Rachel Busbridge, Benjamin Moffitt and Joshua Thorburn, 'Cultural marxism: Far-right conspiracy theory in Australia's culture wars', *Social Identities*, vol. 26, no. 6, pp. 727–28. McKenzie Wark points out that political correctness was imported from the United States, in ways that inverted its meaning. Political correctness was originally 'an expression used by tolerant left-of-centre American academics to sum up precisely the sort of attitude they tried to avoid. In Australia, the thing a sensible leftie would usually eschew is being too "IS" or "ideologically sound" … What was once an ironic bit of self-criticism among leftists was turned into a stick with which to beat them when PC became the slogan of choice for the reorganisation of right-wing attacks against one of their

traditional enemies – the liberal, secular humanities academy' (Wark, *The virtual republic*, p. 156).

32 Jim George and Kim Huynh (eds), *The culture wars: Australian and American politics in the 21st century*, Palgrave Macmillan, South Yarra, 2009.

33 Wark, *The virtual republic*, pp. 156–57.

34 This was part of the Australian Cultural Fields project, funded by the Australian Research Council. The research team was led by Tony Bennett and comprised David Carter, Modesto Gayo, Michelle Kelly, Fred Myers, Greg Noble, David Rowe, Tim Rowse, Deborah Stevenson and Emma Waterton. The major publication from the project is Bennett, Carter, Gayo, Kelly and Noble (eds), *Fields, capital, habitus*.

35 Rowe, Turner and Waterton, 'Introduction', p. 2.

36 Ibid., p. 1.

37 Tony Bennett and David Carter, *Culture in Australia: Policies, publics and programs*, Cambridge University Press, Melbourne, 2001.

38 Rowe, Turner and Waterton, 'Introduction', p. 3.

39 Russell Marks, 'Straight to the pool room: 25 years of *The Castle*', The Monthly, 4 April 2022.

40 Rowe, Turner and Waterton, 'Introduction', p. 5.

41 Rick Morton, 'Negligent to the extreme: Labor inherits crises across por██ ', *The Saturday Paper*, 11–16 June 2022; Michelle Arrow and Frank ██giorno, 'The real "history war" is the attack on our archives and lib██s', *The Sydney Morning Herald*, 16 September 2022.

42 Rowe, Turner and Waterton, 'Introduction', p. 9.

43 Ibid., pp. 10, 11.

44 Justin O'Connor, *After the creative industries: Why we need a cultural economy*, Platform Papers no. 47, Currency House, Strawberry Hills, 2016.

Conclusion: Somewhere in here, there is a better country trying to get out

1 Jacqueline Maley, 'Did the PM pass the pub test? Why we're riveted by politicians' unscripted encounters', *The Sydney Morning Herald*, 10 April 2022.

2 Kelly, *The game*, p. 253.

3 I would argue that the Rudd, Gillard and Turnbull governments were disabled by the same set of forces.

4 Osnos, *Wildland*, p. 324.

5 Kate Jenkins, *Respect@Work: Sexual harassment national inquiry report*, Australian Human Rights Commission, Canberra, 2020.

6 Workplace Gender Equality Agency, 'Australia's gender pay gap statistics', Australian Government, Canberra, 8 March 2022.

7 Julia Baird, *Media tarts: How the Australian press frames female politicians* (revised edition), ABC Books, Sydney, 2021, p. 4.

NOTES

8   Jess Hill, *See what you made me do: Power, control and domestic violence*, Black Inc., Melbourne, 2019.

9   Louise Milligan, *Witness: An investigation into the brutal cost of seeking justice*, Hachette, Melbourne, 2021.

10   Baird, *Media tarts*, p. 24.

11   Ellis, *Sex, lies and question time*, p. 3

12   Jackie Huggins, *Sister girl: Reflections on Tiddaism, identity and reconciliation* (revised edition), University of Queensland Press, St Lucia, 2022.

13   Kirstie Wellauer and Bridget Brennan, 'Vote Compass data finds the most Australians support Indigenous Voice to Parliament – and it has grown since the last election', ABC News, 4 May 2022.

14   Graeme Turner, 'Dealing with diversity: Australian television, homogeneity and indigeneity', *Media International Australia*, vol. 174, no. 1, p. 21.

15   Ben Dibley and Graeme Turner, 'Indigeneity, cosmopolitanism and the nation: the project of NITV', in Rowe, Turner and Waterton (eds), *Making culture*, pp. 132–33.

16   Natasha Kassam and Hannah Léser, *Climate poll 2021*, Lowy Institute, Sydney, 26 May 2021, www.lowyinstitute.org/publications/climate-poll-2021.

17   Ipsos, *The Ipsos climate change report 2022*, Ipsos, 2022.

18   Wilkinson, *The carbon club*.

19   Adam Morton and Graham Readfearn, 'State of the environment: Shocking report shows how Australia's land and wildlife are being destroyed', *The Guardian*, 19 July 2022.

20   For those who have not watched it, *Gogglebox* shows a selection of households in which the inhabitants (singles, couples and families) simply watch television. Their responses to the programs they view provide the content for the show, and are often funny and insightful. Routinely disrespectful, these views show us what people *really* think about the television they watch, as they watch it.

21   Keane, *The mess we're in*, p. 261; Denniss, *Big*, p. 1; Megalogenis, 'Exit strategy', pp. 70–71.

22   Denniss, *Dead right*, p. ix.

23   Australia Institute, 'Profits causing inflation in Australia, not wages: European Central Bank and ABS data reveals', media release, 18 July 2022.

24   Wayne Errington and Peter van Onselen, *Victory: The inside story of Labor's return to power*, HarperCollins, Sydney, 2022.

25   Jessica Irvine, 'Labor should stick with stage three tax cuts, but on one condition', *The Sydney Morning Herald*, 1 November 2022.

227

Selected major sources

Full bibliographic information on all sources cited can be found within the relevant endnotes.

Benedict Anderson, *Imagined communities: Reflections on the origin and spread of nationalism*, Verso, London, 1983.

Mark Andrejevic, *Infoglut: How too much information is changing the way we think and know*, Routledge, New York and London, 2013.

—— *Automated media*, Routledge, New York and London, 2019.

Julia Baird, *Media tarts: How the Australian press frames female politicians* (revised edition), ABC Books, Sydney, 2021.

Sarah Banet-Weiser, *Authentic: The politics of ambivalence in a brand culture*, New York University Press, New York and London, 2012.

Tony Bennett and David Carter, *Culture in Australia: Policies, publics and programs*, Cambridge University Press, Melbourne, 2001.

Tony Bennett, David Carter, Modesto Gayo, Michelle Kelly and Greg Noble (eds), *Fields, capitals, habitus: Australian culture, inequalities and social divisions*, Routledge, London and New York, 2021.

Judith Brett, *Doing politics: Writing on public life*, Text, Melbourne, 2021.

Nick Bryant, *The rise and fall of Australia: How a great nation lost its way*, Bantam, Sydney, 2014.

Taina Bucher, *If ... then: Algorithmic power and politics*, Oxford University Press, New York, 2018.

—— *Facebook*, Polity, Cambridge, 2022.

Craig Calhoun, *Nations matter: Culture, history, and the cosmopolitan dream*, Routledge, London and New York, 2007.

Damien Cave, *Into the rip: How the Australian way of risk made my family, stronger, happier ... and less American*, Scribner, Sydney, 2021.

Gabrielle Chan, *Rusted off: Why country Australia is fed up*, Vintage, Sydney, 2018.

SELECTED MAJOR SOURCES

Jonathan Cohn, *The burden of choice: Recommendations, subversion, and algorithmic culture*, Rutgers University Press, New Brunswick, 2019.

Paul Collier and John Kay, *Greed is dead: Politics after individualism*, Allen Lane, London, 2020.

Stefan Collini, *What are universities for?*, Penguin, London, 2012.

Ed Coper, *Facts and other lies: Welcome to the disinformation age*, Allen & Unwin, Sydney, 2022.

Kate Crawford, *Atlas of AI: Power, politics and the planetary costs of artificial intelligence*, Yale University Press, New Haven, 2021.

Stuart Cunningham and David Craig, *Social media entertainment: The new intersection of Hollywood and Silicon Valley*, New York University Press, New York, 2019.

John Daley, *Gridlock: Removing barriers to policy reform*, Grattan Institute, Melbourne, 2021.

Richard Denniss, *Dead right: How neoliberalism ate itself and what comes next*, Black Inc., Melbourne, 2019.

—— *Big: The role of the state in the modern economy*, Monash University Publishing, Melbourne, 2022.

Keith Dowding, *It's the government, stupid: How governments blame citizens for their own policies*, Bristol University Press, Bristol, 2020.

Kate Ellis, *Sex, lies and question time: Why the successes and struggles of women in Australia's parliament matters to us all*, Hardie Grant, Melbourne, 2021.

Wayne Errington and Peter van Onselen, *How good is Scott Morrison?*, Hachette, Sydney, 2021.

—— 2022, *Victory: The inside story of Labor's return to power*, HarperCollins, Sydney, 2022.

Virginia Eubanks, *Automating inequality: How high-tech tools profile, police, and punish the poor*, St Martin's Press, New York, 2018.

Terry Flew, Petros Iosifidis and Jeanette Steemers (eds), *Global media and national policies: The return of the state*, Palgrave Macmillan, London, 2016.

Hannah Forsyth, *A history of the modern Australian university*, NewSouth, Sydney, 2014.

Jim George and Kim Huynh (eds), *The culture wars: Australian and American politics in the 21st century*, Palgrave Macmillan, South Yarra, 2009.

Andreas Hepp, *Cultures of mediatization*, Polity, London, 2013.

Jess Hill, *See what you made me do: Power, control and domestic violence*, Black Inc., Melbourne, 2019.

Ken Hillis, Michael Petit and Kylie Jarrett, *Google and the culture of search*, Routledge, London and New York, 2013.

Jackie Huggins, *Sister girl: Reflections on Tiddaism, identity and reconciliation* (revised edition), University of Queensland Press, St Lucia, 2022.

Ken Inglis, *Whose ABC? The Australian Broadcasting Corporation 1983–2006*, Black Inc., Melbourne, 2006.

Nadia Kaneva (ed.), *Branding post-communist nations: Marketizing national identities in the 'new' Europe*, Routledge, New York, 2012.

Bernard Keane, *The mess we're in: How our politics went to hell and dragged us with it*, Allen & Unwin, Sydney, 2018.

—— *Lies and falsehoods: The Morrison government and the culture of deceit*, Hardie Grant, Melbourne, 2021.

Sean Kelly, *The game: A portrait of Scott Morrison*, Black Inc., Melbourne, 2021.

Stephanie Kelton, *The deficit myth: Modern monetary theory and how to build a better economy*, John Murray, London, 2020.

Steven Levitsky and Daniel Ziblatt, *How democracies die: What history reveals about our future*, Viking, New York, 2018.

Stuart Macintyre, André Brett and Gwilym Croucher, *No end of a lesson: Australia's unified system of higher education*, Melbourne University Press, Melbourne, 2017.

Stuart Macintyre and Anna Clark, *The history wars*, Melbourne University Press, Melbourne, 2003.

Simon Marginson and Mark Considine, *The enterprise university: Power, governance and reinvention in Australia*, Cambridge University Press, Cambridge, 2000.

David Marr and Marian Wilkinson, *Dark victory: How a government lied its way to political triumph*, Allen & Unwin, Sydney, 2003.

Jim McGuigan, *Cool capitalism*, Pluto, London, 2009.

David McKnight, *Populism now! The case for progressive populism*, NewSouth, Sydney, 2018.

Brian McNair, Terry Flew, Stephen Harrington and Adam Swift, *Politics, media and democracy in Australia: Public and producer perceptions of the political public sphere*, Routledge, London, 2017.

George Megalogenis, *Faultlines: Race, work and the politics of changing Australia*, Scribe, Melbourne, 2003.

—— *Australia's second chance: What our history tells us about our future*, Hamish Hamilton, Sydney, 2015.

—— 'Balancing act: Australia between recession and renewal', *Quarterly Essay*, 61, Black Inc., Melbourne, 2016.

—— 'Exit strategy: Politics after the pandemic', *Quarterly Essay*, 82, Black Inc., Melbourne, 2021.

Sabina Mihelj, *Media nations: Communicating belonging and exclusion in the modern world*, Palgrave Macmillan, London, 2011.

Louise Milligan, *Witness: An investigation into the brutal cost of seeking justice*, Hachette, Melbourne, 2021.

Anthony Moran, *Australia: Nation, belonging, and globalization*, Routledge, New York and London, 2005.

Tom Nichols, *The death of expertise: The campaign against established knowledge and why it matters*, Oxford University Press, New York, 2017.

SELECTED MAJOR SOURCES

Katharine Murphy, 'Lone wolf: Albanese and the new politics', *Quarterly Essay*, 88, 2022.

Justin O'Connor, *After the creative industries: Why we need a cultural economy*, Platform Papers no. 47, Currency House, Strawberry Hills, 2016.

Evan Osnos, *Wildland: The making of America's fury*, Bloomsbury, New York, 2021.

Eli Pariser, *The filter bubble: What the internet is hiding from you*, Penguin, New York, 2011.

Aaron Patrick, *Downfall: How the Labor Party ripped itself apart*, ABC Books, Sydney, 2013.

Anna Cristina Pertierra and Graeme Turner, *Locating television: Zones of consumption*, Routledge, London and New York, 2013.

Thomas Piketty (translated by Arthur Goldhammer), *Capital in the twenty-first century*, Belknap Press of Harvard University Press, Cambridge MA, 2014.

Michael Pusey, *Economic rationalism in Canberra: A nation building state changes its mind*, Cambridge University Press, Melbourne, 1991.

—— *The experience of middle Australia: The dark side of economic reform*, Cambridge University Press, Melbourne, 2003.

John Quiggin, 'Dismembering government: New public management and why the Commonwealth government can't do anything anymore', *The Monthly*, September 2021.

Robert Reich, *The common good*, Vintage, New York, 2018.

Howard Rheingold, *The virtual community: Homesteading on the electronic frontier* (revised edition), MIT Press, Cambridge MA, 2000.

Matthew Ricketson and Patrick Mullins, *Who needs the ABC? Why taking it for granted is no longer an option*, Scribe, Melbourne, 2022.

David Rowe, Graeme Turner and Emma Waterton (eds), *Making culture: Commercialisation, transnationalism, and the state of 'nationing' in contemporary Australia*, Routledge, London and New York, 2018.

Niki Savva, *The road to ruin: How Tony Abbott and Peta Credlin destroyed their own government*, Scribe, Melbourne, 2016.

—— *Plots and prayers: Malcolm Turnbull's demise and Scott Morrison's ascension*, Scribe, Melbourne, 2019.

—— *Bulldozed: Scott Morrison's fall and Anthony Albanese's rise*, Scribe, Melbourne, 2022.

Cass Sunstein, *Republic.com 2.0*, Princeton University Press, Princeton, 2009.

Lindsay Tanner, *Sideshow: Dumbing down democracy*, Scribe, Melbourne, 2011.

Steven Threadgold and Jessica Gerrard (eds), *Class in Australia*, Monash University Publishing, Melbourne, 2022.

Rodney Tiffen, *Disposable leaders: Media and leadership coups from Menzies to Abbott*, NewSouth, Sydney, 2017.

Laura Tingle, 'Political amnesia: How we forgot how to govern', *Quarterly*

Essay, 60, Black Inc., Melbourne, 2015.

—— 'Follow the leader: Democracy and the rise of the strongman', *Quarterly Essay*, 71, Black Inc., Melbourne, 2018.

Graeme Turner, *Making it national: Nationalism and Australian popular culture*, Allen & Unwin, Sydney, 1994.

—— *Ending the affair: The decline of television current affairs in Australia*, UNSW Press, Sydney, 2005.

—— *Ordinary people and the media: The demotic turn*, Sage, London, 2010.

—— *Re-inventing the media*, Routledge, London and New York, 2016.

Graeme Turner, Frances Bonner and P. David Marshall, *Fame games: The production of celebrity in Australia*, Cambridge University Press, Melbourne, 2000.

José van Dijck, Thomas Poell and Martijn de Waal, *The platform society: Public values in a connected world*, Oxford University Press, New York, 2018.

Zala Volcic and Mark Andrejevic (eds), *Commercial nationalism: Selling the nation and nationalizing the sell*, Palgrave Macmillan, London, 2016.

McKenzie Wark, *The virtual republic: Australia's culture wars of the 1990s*, Allen & Unwin, Sydney, 1997.

Marian Wilkinson, *The carbon club: How a network of influential climate sceptics, politicians and business leaders fought to control Australia's climate policy*, Allen & Unwin, Sydney, 2020.

George Yúdice, 'Community', in Tony Bennett, Lawrence Grossberg and Meaghan Morris (eds), *New keywords: A revised vocabulary of culture and society*, Blackwell, Malden, MA, 2001, pp. 51–53.

Shoshana Zuboff, *The age of surveillance capitalism: The fight for a human future at the new frontier of power*, Public Affairs, New York, 2019.